"As someone who has kept a journal or notebook for much of my life and who has facilitated classes in keeping a notebook, I found Donna Bearden's book, *Finding More Me: Journaling to go Soul Deep,* a wonderful resource not only for beginning writers/artists but also for those of us who think we know everything there is to know about keeping a journal. Donna's book is neither prescriptive, nor rule centered. She gives the reader guidelines, methods, tools to aid with the 'journaling journey.' She shares her personal experiences to help readers write theirs. This book offers a creative challenge for all readers who are interested in finding a more authentic way to be in the world, to discover the power of words and images to change lives."

—Anita Skeen
Professor Emerita, Founding Director, RCAH Center for Poetry, Michigan State University

"*Finding More Me: Journaling to Go Soul Deep* is a profound book of personal exploration, yet it is so much more than that. Whether you've done journal writing all your life or are new to the practice, you will find within these pages practical and accessible ways to transform yourself. Donna Bearden, a true soul explorer, does just that. She shares her own stories, her pains and her struggles, and shows us how she used the practices of journal writing to bring herself to wholeness. The beautifully written stories are compelling unto themselves, one could almost say spell-binding, and she skillfully uses them as context to make the techniques real. If you are dealing with unresolved issues, have not been able to free yourself from your own demons, and truly desire to live more fully, this book is for you."

—Gail Hollander
Artist, Workshop Creator and Facilitator

"A wondrous journey into the world of journaling. Donna takes us by the hand and guides us to the pen, the paper and the inspiration to act. Carl Jung once said, 'Until you make the unconscious conscious, it will direct your life and you will call it fate.' Donna offers us a beautiful opportunity to turn fate into simple practices that give us access to our shadow selves."

—Andy Chaleff
Author, *The Last Letter: Embracing Pain to Create a Meaningful Life*

"What? Journaling isn't the same as keeping a diary? I knew this, but never considered how powerful the difference can be. Donna Bearden's *Finding More Me* is a crash course in uncovering the internal messages that continue to creep into your life, causing damage to all relationships, especially the one with yourself. By sharing her own personal stories with heart-opening vulnerability, readers have a path to follow that will undoubtably contribute to a much lighter, more intentional future."

—Sarah Elkins
Author, *Your Stories Don't Define You: How You Tell Them Will*

"As an on-and-off journaler who has always wanted to be more on, I'm beyond excited for this fountain of inspiration from Donna Bearden! I've known the author long enough to know that she *knows* this stuff, she *does* it, and she knows how to share it. Instead of telling us what we ought to do to go 'soul deep,' she invites us, with her beautiful compassionate energy, to explore the practices that she practices, to drink from the waters that give her such rich awareness and insight. This book is an extraordinary gift of the heart to the world."

—Rebecca Dwight Bruff
Author, *Trouble the Water*

"Donna Bearden's *Finding More Me: Journaling to Go Soul Deep* is not a read it and think about it book. It's a read it and put it into action book. There is an undeniable art to letting go and moving on. *Finding More Me* gives the extra incentive to do just that. Donna probes deeply into harsh realities of past pain but doesn't leave us in a lurch. Instead she offers concrete ideas through writing, drawing, and creating mandalas from photographs or pictures. The practice of these arts grants personal insight and healing, allowing the reader freedom to embrace whatever comes next with energy and exuberance."

—Donna Keel Armer
Author, *Solo in Salento: A Memoir*

"From years of experience walking her own inner journey, Donna Bearden, in her newest book, sets forth a feast of possibilities for anyone pondering or experienced in the practice of journal writing. With grit and openness, Donna sets a table with a wide-open invitation to explore our inner conversation, saying with each course, *take your time, do not rush the process, listen for answers, be kind to yourself. Finding More Me* will stay off my shelf and find a home by my side, as I continue to work toward finding new paths and courage to welcome myself to my own table of discovery."

—Dr. Jean M. Richardson
Executive Director, Kirkridge Retreat and Study Center

"In her book, *Finding More Me: Journaling to Go Soul Deep*, Donna Bearden creates a new map for the process of journaling, one with trails for deeper knowledge of the soul, healing, redemption, and especially for exploring alternate ways of being in the world. By including guidelines for using mandalas, collage, and photography, she enhances the experience of journaling with manifold opportunities to examine the paths that have shaped one's life. Her writing is lucid, authentic, and a promising invitation to engage in a deeper discussion with oneself."

—Pam Noble
Author, *Becoming Tree: Mystical Wanderings in Nature Through Essays, Poems, and Art*

"What immediately strikes me in *Finding More Me* is that there's something for everyone in this treasure of a book—or rather, in this exquisite invitation. We're beckoned through one hundred different doors to commune more deeply, through journaling, with who we really are and in whatever ways feel serving of our best selves. With Donna Bearden's help, we can't possibly say no! And we can't help but find more of ourselves, too."

—Sue M. Brightman
Author, *A Call to Further Becoming: The New Declaration from Women Over 50*

Finding More Me:
Journaling to Go Soul Deep

by Donna Bearden

ISBN 978-1-64663-105-6

Published by

◄ köehlerbooks™

3705 Shore Drive
Virginia Beach, VA 23455
800–435–4811
www.koehlerbooks.com

FINDING MORE

ME

JOURNALING TO GO
SOUL DEEP

Donna Bearden

VIRGINIA BEACH
CAPE CHARLES

For Elaine.

TABLE OF CONTENTS

I'm standing on the outside of my life looking in and wondering what it would be like if I had the courage to show up and let myself be seen.
Brené Brown

FOREWORD

I, too, have stood on the outside of my life looking in. I, too, would like the courage to show up and let myself be seen. But first I have to figure out who I am. Writing helps me do that. I don't know if I'll ever totally figure me out. The good news is that I'm getting closer and closer to having the courage to let myself be seen, and I give a lot of credit to journaling.

Much of my life has been about listening to other people. I paid close attention to what others believed and how they acted. I wanted to fit in, to be accepted, to belong. A sense of belonging is a primary need and motivator, and thus we inevitably adopt the beliefs and habits of the people who care for us. We have layers and layers of beliefs, traditions, rules, expectations, myths, stories, dreams, and knowledge, much of it in the form of unchallenged assumptions.

In my desire to belong, I often felt I was wearing a mask and playing a role in someone else's story. Journaling was my way into the deepest part of me and my way out into the world in a more authentic way. Who was I beneath others' expectations?

I asked it over and over in various ways and allowed my pen to say some surprising things to me. So many layers to explore. As I became clearer through my journaling, I discarded layers that defined who I thought I was supposed to be, and discovered layers that expressed the soul-deep me. It wasn't quick and easy. It's still not quick and easy. It takes perseverance, persistence, and time. Maybe a lifetime.

REASONS I JOURNAL:

The number one reason I journal is to listen to the deepest part of me, and to gain clarity on what I believe underneath what I *think* I believe.

I journal because I am easily distracted. Some people can figure things out through their thought processes alone. My mind wanders so easily that I need the physical act of writing, or drawing, or photographing to help keep me focused. I need the involvement of pen on paper to stick to the point. If I don't have that, my thinking mimics my internet searching. One thing leads to another and circles through a dozen distractions. A couple hours pass and I'm no closer to an answer.

I journal to invite synchronicity into my life. Synchronicity is when two or more events happen close together, are meaningfully connected, and seem to be more than coincidence. You think of someone and they call. You ask a question and a book shows up with the answer. Most of us have had those types of experiences. I have found that when I journal about specific questions, answers come from the most unexpected places: songs, books, a gift, a phone call, a stranger. There's something about asking a question, setting an intention, focusing on an area of interest that invites the universe to respond.

Most importantly, I journal because it's meditative, calming and relaxing. I have learned that I'm more centered and more peaceful when I write. For me, it's a lifeline to an intelligent, calming voice that seems much wiser than I am. Some would say it's the god within. Artists and writers have described an underground river they tap into, or ideas that come through them. There are times I feel that, and it's both exciting and humbling. It happens more and more as I show up regularly, same time, same ritual, different methods.

In this book, I hope to share my journaling journey with you. Chapter 1 is the stuff you may already know and adhere to. It contains the guidelines I use for journaling, the rules I've found helpful, the mechanics. Read it or skim it. It's the basic information just to be sure we're all on the same page. If your journaling routine is firmly established and you're happy with it, skip over it and dive into the good stuff in the chapters that follow.

I've used many methods of journaling, and each one has helped me in a different way. I could simply describe each of these techniques, and this would be a very dry book indeed. I will share some personal stories with you as examples in order to convey the power of the process.

Each chapter will present a method, or two when they're intertwined, and will give examples of what they've taught me. My aim is to give you an overview of several tools and to encourage you to try them all. If you're drawn to a certain method and want to go deeper, there are experts who can lead you further. I will name a few (and apologize to those whose work I haven't encountered yet).

There is no strict order to the chapters. I'm going to hit the heaviest stuff first, the methods that took me deeper than anything else. Then we'll lighten up a bit and talk about some other techniques. Pick and choose. You may want to try the lighter stuff first. It's up to you. Try whatever you think will be helpful. If you're drawn to visual journaling with collage, turn to chapter 5. If you want to work with shadows and archetypes, go to chapter 3. If you're curious about mandalas and how they might fit in with journaling, read chapter 2. If you want to have some wordplay fun, turn to the thesaurus game in chapter 4. I use one method for a while and then another. Sometimes I use more than one at a time. Think of the book as a handbook. Turn to what you want to learn at the time you want to learn it. Refer to the Resources at the back of the book for some basic journaling methods that are also helpful but don't require in-depth explanations.

But first, an important clarification. There is a difference between journaling and writing a memoir.

Writing a memoir is telling my life story, maybe in sequence, maybe by themes, maybe by many other methods. It's recalling and putting meaning to the things that happened in my life. Explaining my life.

Journaling also comes from my experiences and the meaning I find in them. But it's more about today. What do I believe? What do I see? What helps me go deeper into my deepest self and ask the question *Who am I?*

Yes, I go into the past. Yes, I tell stories. Yes, I look at themes. Yes, I recall and put meaning to the things that happened in my life. But I'm not trying to tell a story with a beginning, a middle, and an end. Nor am I documenting what happened day by day as I did long ago in my first diaries.

In journaling, I'm having an ongoing discussion with myself, a wondering about so many different things. A wandering down so many paths and possibilities.

To summarize, I journal in order to
- listen to the deepest part of me
- gain clarity on what I believe underneath what I think I believe
- keep my wandering, easily distracted mind focused
- invite synchronicity into my life
- stay more centered and calm

I have learned, on my journeys, that if I let a day go by without writing, I grow uneasy. Two days and I am in tremor. Three and I suspect lunacy.
Ray Bradbury

CHAPTER 1: JOURNALING GUIDELINES

Whether you are an experienced journaler or just beginning, the guidelines in this chapter are worth reviewing. In the end, define your own guidelines, the ones most helpful to you.

Start with the Big Question:

What should I do with old journals?

Those Pesky Old Journals

I don't believe there's any way to short-cut the excavating of issues, muck and compost. I certainly couldn't, and so I have dozens of journals filled with my wonderings and wanderings. I have worked hard to understand the family and the times I was born into. It has been complex, complicated, and confusing. Devastating at times. I have looked for reason, for secrets to understanding human nature and motivation. It's all there in many notebooks filled with words and stories and struggles, important to no one but me, a record of my growth. Would I want it to be common knowledge? Probably not.

The big question, then, is what to do with journals I have

poured my heart and soul into. What if I die and someone has to clean out my closets? Can I be honest on the page if I fear someone finding out I was not exactly the sweet, considerate person they thought I was? This question often prevents people from journaling and needs to be addressed right up front.

Establish an agreement with someone you trust so you know without a shadow of a doubt that you can write honestly and openly. Some years ago, I gave the responsibility to my daughter: *When I die, go to the closet, pull out all the journals and burn them.* She reminded me of that pact recently. (Was I looking particularly tired that day?) With this agreement in place, I can continue to write, knowing my questions, my rantings and ravings, my shadows and rough edges will not be exposed. I need this freedom to explore my deepest thoughts and feelings.

Time, Place, and Ritual

So many writers repeat the mantra of same time, same place, that it's worth trying. But in the end, do what works for you and your life right now. We're all at different stages with a variety of causes and issues tugging at our sleeves.

My ritual is this: I wake up early, make myself a cup of tea in my favorite cup, and go to my reading/writing chair—which *IS* a dedicated reading/writing chair, not a workstation or a computer chair, or a place I talk on the phone or do anything else besides journal or read. I take a few sips of tea and a few deep breaths, pick up my journal, and set an intention for writing, often by asking a question. I used to light a candle until one morning the smoke set off the fire alarm. Now I'm too worried and distracted it might happen again. The ideal is to reduce all distractions.

I haven't always had the luxury of writing every morning. I certainly couldn't afford that luxury when working and raising kids. Back then, I had to snatch moments when kids were in bed or get up in the middle of the night when a question or idea wouldn't leave me alone. There are huge gaps in my life when I didn't write, or at least not consistently. Life was too busy, too chaotic, too hectic. If you are in one of those time periods, don't add one more commitment just because you think it's a good idea. At some point, even good commitments can become one more thing on a to-do list. Be kind to yourself. If it's helpful, do it. If it's one more stressor in a stressed and stretched life, don't.

Journals and Pens

Fancy journals are beautiful, inviting, nice to hold, and can be intimidating as hell. When I sit down with an expensive journal, my internal editor-in-chief sits right down beside me with his red pencil behind his ear, eager to "help" me by proof-reading. I cannot put the first sentence on the page without making sure all my i's are dotted, my t's are crossed, and my grammar is impeccable. And I use big words like "impeccable" so he'll smile at my intelligence.

Don't get me wrong. I LOVE beautiful journals. I buy them from time to time. I'm delighted if someone gives me one. But it's taken a lifetime to learn to write in them! For the longest time, even with good intentions, I used them only for special occasions or retreats. Then there they would sit with four to ten pages of lonely writing. Maybe fancy journals represented what I aspired to, words so well spoken, so true in meaning they deserved to be in beautiful bindings. Journals are rough drafts, not published best sellers.

Finally, I learned to tell my editor-in-chief to take a hike. I can use an inexpensive spiral notebook, or notebook paper and a three-ring binder, or give myself permission to be messy and imperfect in a beautiful journal. Experiment with what works best for you. Size, quality of paper, lined or unlined. Use something that doesn't intimidate you, something that invites you to get messy and doesn't care if you misspell words or use bad grammar.

While you might choose cheaper notebooks until you accept messy as part of the process, don't skimp on pens. Find pens that feel good in your hand, glide easily across the page, and don't leave gaps or smudges. I love gel pens. I love colored pens, especially turquoise and purple. I want a whole set of colored pens sitting at wacky angles at my elbow. I like using many colors and doodling in margins.

Confidentiality

Establish confidentiality with yourself. Truly! Confidentiality is absolutely necessary to get down through the layers to the YOU within. Treat your inner YOU as the dearest friend you have, the one who can say anything and trust you to keep confidence. When your friend is telling you a heart-wrenching story, you do not interrupt to correct grammar or change a word, and you do not run to tell someone else. You listen. You listen deeply. You don't try to fix anything. You just listen. That's the writing you will do. You will not edit as you write and will not share your writing with anyone else. The YOU-inside needs to trust the you-with-the-pen. You are writing to invite the deepest part of you to show up. Dismiss your critic. Do not judge, evaluate, or analyze as you write.

Spiral Learning

We learn in a spiral kind of way, circling back to an idea, maybe a little further down the path, but having to revisit an idea time and time again to get it. I used to say I was a slow learner, but now I'm kinder to myself and acknowledge how difficult it is to change a belief or a defense mechanism that is automatic and unconscious until something happens to bring it forward.

You've probably noticed people who seem to make the same "mistakes" over and over and find themselves in similar situations as the one they just got out of. Oops, maybe that person is me.

The universe seems to present me with the same challenge again and again until I learn to respond differently, or I see something in myself I hadn't acknowledged, or, as you'll see in the next chapter, I own the emotions I was trying to hide.

That spiral also appears in almost any learning path we find ourselves on. Knowledge and understanding build year by year. Wisdom comes only with experience.

Summary

- Decide what to do with old journals and who's responsible if . . . you know.
- Dedicate a time and place for journaling, *or*
- Snatch time whenever possible.
- Develop a simple ritual that sets the stage and helps you focus.
- Eliminate as many distractions as possible.
- Establish confidentiality with yourself.
- Do not edit as you write.
- Use an inviting notebook (spiral, notebook paper, fancy journal) and a good pen.
- Learning occurs in a spiral as we circle back to ideas and find ourselves a little further down the path.

Part 1
The Heavy Stuff

No tears in the writer, no tears in the reader. No surprise in the writer, no surprise in the reader.
Robert Frost

CHAPTER 2: FOUR-DAY WRITES AND PHOTO MANDALAS

Each of these practices, four-day writes and photo mandalas, is powerful and can stand on its own. They happened simultaneously for me and were so interwoven that I want to present them together. The writing told me one thing, the visual another.

While writing has always been my go-to when trying to figure out my feelings, and has always helped me get clearer, it wasn't until I worked with a very wise counselor who assigned a specific way of writing that I broke through a major stuck place. I found tears that had not been shed, emotions that had not been felt. I had some lifelong issues I needed to work through in order to move forward. I had worked hard on my issues over the years, but there were still emotional responses that clung to me like gum on the bottom of a shoe, automatic responses that kept me safe and protected from perceived threats.

Each of us develops early beliefs and habits based on the world in which we find ourselves. Some become defense mechanisms to help us survive. Some grow impenetrable and we continue to use them even when they are no longer helpful. My defense, for example, was *busyness,* and it became an addiction.

I was addicted to busyness so completely I would panic if I had too much unstructured time. Nothing scared me more than an empty square on my calendar, unless it was two squares side by side.

I wish I were kidding. I'm not. I learned early that the best way to deal with my life was to get as busy as possible, stay away from home as much as possible, and never let anyone catch me sitting idle. I learned that busyness kept emotions (and people) at bay. Unstructured free time, on the other hand, invited a trip down a deep, dark well.

After a lifetime of this habit, I went to see a wise and intuitive counselor named Elaine Sullivan. I was tired of being busy to the point of compulsion but didn't know how to slow down without going into depression. The old story came out quickly. Authoritarian, perfectionist, intellectual father. Withdrawn, depressed mother. A family secret kept well hidden. I had learned early to stay busy because achievement was highly valued.

The Assignment

Elaine gave me an assignment: a four-day write, based on the work of James Pennebaker. Serendipitously, I had just heard an interview with Dr. Pennebaker on NPR. A psychologist at the University of Texas in Austin, he has researched the power of writing in connection with trauma. Elaine didn't have to convince me of his methods. She just outlined the steps.

Write for four days in a row about the issue, at least twenty minutes each day with no interruptions.

Say whatever comes to mind. Anything.

Do not edit as you write.

Do not share what you write.

Elaine made it clear I wasn't to do the assignment until I could write for four days in a row. "I warn you," she said, "the third day will be rough." I didn't believe her about the third day, but she was right. Day 3 was hard.

Part 1 of my assignment was the writing. Part 2 was something I added myself.

The Artwork

About a month earlier, I had read about the psychologist Carl Jung's use of mandalas. For about two years, Jung drew mandalas every morning as a means of accessing the subconscious. In my curiosity to learn more, I stumbled onto websites showing mandalas made from photographs. I am an avid photographer and was instantly drawn in. I kept searching until I found a site that explained how to create photo mandalas. It didn't take long for this new art form to become a regular practice. The process is calming and meditative. (See Part 3 for instructions.)

During my early work with mandalas, I purposely didn't read about their history, their interpretations, their use in various cultures. I didn't want to put any parameters or expectations on my own explorations. I wanted to allow whatever happened to happen. It was an art form, a meditation, a way for me to create a calming space for the raw feelings coming up in my writing. As with the kaleidoscopes I played with as a kid, mandalas drew me into a quiet space of reflection.

I combined the mandala-making with my four-day write assignments. Each day I would write, usually much longer than the prescribed twenty minutes. Then I would go to the computer and create a mandala. On the first two days, I knew in advance the photograph I wanted to work with. On the last two days, I scrolled through the files and let a photograph choose me. Something in the picture matched something I was feeling.

For four days I wrote and created mandalas. Each day was powerful and revealing. At the end of the four days, I was spent, physically and emotionally. A critical guideline for the writing is that it is done for your eyes only. At the end of the four days, you choose what to do with the pages—burn them, shred them, save them in a safe place. Your choice. This understanding gives the writer permission to put down on paper whatever comes up. It allowed me to feel feelings I had not allowed myself to feel, and to say things about my feelings. Raw, angry, scary feelings that led to raw, angry, scary words.

When I say I was angry, it came from a deep, deep place in me. When I say I was sad, it was my very toes that cried. It was easy to hate. I had often stopped there. It was harder to open the adjoining door to longing, loneliness, the need to be touched, the need to be held when I was upset. The extremes of the two-year-old. These were the feelings I felt. Big scary feelings I was scolded for, sent to my room for, told to get under control. Big scary feelings I had locked securely away in order to be acceptable. I wrote some big, bad, ugly words in those four days. Feelings spilled out of me I didn't know were there. Words tumbled out I didn't know I could say.

The writing and photo mandalas went like this:

Day 1 Writing

I didn't want to write so bad that my ear hurt, my throat hurt, my arm hurt, and my fingers were cramped. That's how bad I didn't want to write. I made myself sit down with pen and paper, and somehow the words began coming. I wrote for an hour or so.

I feared my father growing up. I stayed out of his way as much as possible. He had a hair-trigger temper that could blow with the slightest provocation. He could rip anyone apart with his words, his logic, and his coldness. I got very good at reading body language and tiptoeing on eggshells. I tried to understand him. I didn't know where his anger came from. I thought perhaps it was selfishness since he grew up an only child. Or maybe it was his work that was so important and stressful. Maybe it was too many kids and too much responsibility. But until I was eighteen, I didn't know about his first wife who died and was never spoken of again. She was a secret kept so well hidden that I never suspected my two oldest brothers had a different mother. His bottled-up grief and disappointments poured out toxin on children who were too loud or too quiet, didn't know correct answers or pronunciations, made Bs instead of As.

There was the nightly grilling at the dinner table where each child was asked questions. If we knew the first answer, he would ask more and more difficult questions and then shame us for not knowing the answers. He seemed more interested in showing off his own knowledge than trying to help us learn anything. It felt like being pinned down by a giant opponent, a daily reminder that we weren't so smart, followed by the ever-repeated question, "What am I sending you to school for?" No, wait. It was probably "Why am I sending you to school?" because you didn't dare end a sentence with a preposition. My father was an engineer, a meticulous pianist, and had once worked as an editor. Dinnertime was not pleasant. Sometimes the smallest wrong answer would be enough to exasperate him into an explosion worthy of the idiot children before him.

My mother had been a woman ahead of her time; she taught college and had become one of the first woman officers in the Navy. During the war, she worked side by side with my father in an office in Washington DC. She married him, took on his two young children and bore him five more. In addition to the grilling of the children, dinnertime was also used for subtle put-downs of my mother. I am not blameless. He brought me into his pricks. He once offered a reward to the child who could find out how much she weighed. I took up the challenge, spied on her to learn where she wrote it down, and got a quarter for my Judas betrayal. I'm not proud of it, and even knew at the time that I was scum for doing something underhanded just to get his fleeting approval.

He took a piece of my soul, and I wanted it back. I was tired of the hold he still had on me.

The kind of writing done in a four-day write is free flowing with one idea leading to another like water seeping into cracks. My father having a "hold on me" led to "hold me." And I wondered if he ever did. Maybe he held me, hugged me, put his arms around me when I was a baby. I don't remember being held. I don't remember any hugging in my family.

And that reminded me of a family I hated to sit behind at church. The father, Paul, adored his children. He put his arms around them, whispered to them, right there in front of God and everyone. He wasn't proper at all. He didn't seem to care if people knew that he loved his kids. It hurt something deep inside me when I sat behind that family. It was all I could do to keep the tears in my eyes where they belonged. One time, Paul brought his five-year-old son over when he came to get a bookcase. He let the little guy help. I couldn't believe it. That kid wasn't in the way at all. He was a genuine helper and was so proud to be included.

But my father never had that kind of time. He was too busy, you see, and it was faster and more efficient to do it himself than have kids in the way slowing him down.

I kept writing that first day. My writing was sarcastic, mean, hateful, vengeful, spiteful. There was no leniency whatsoever. It was my wicked witch speaking, cackling, demanding equal time, pointing a long bony finger. The words kept coming. The accusations. The hurts. The shaming. The put-downs. It all spilled out on that paper as I wrote faster and faster and the handwriting got bigger and bigger and sloppier and sloppier. I knew I was being one-sided. I knew I wasn't giving him any leeway at all. But that had been part of the problem. I had spent far too much time making excuses for him, trying to explain away his behavior, putting meaning to it, trying to understand it and him. I think they call it "intellectualizing." I was very good at that. I grew up in an intellectual family. The problem was that I had never, never listened to the little girl in pigtails who felt betrayed and abandoned even by her own grown-up self. This was not an intellectual essay to turn in for a grade. This was a purging.

I hated him.

But at the same time, I wanted him to love me. I wanted him to see me for who I was, not someone who was a constant disappointment.

I kept writing.

And another thing. . .

And another. . .

And another. . .

"I'm getting braver," I wrote. "He will be silent. He will not lift a finger or even an eyebrow because, you see, he is dead. This is my last effort to sweep out the lingering effects of what he did to my soul, my little girl, my adult woman, my artist, my warrior, my gentle self. My words will come out and the grammar will undoubtedly be wrong, and I may say one word when I mean another. And incomplete sentences. Subjects with no verbs. Or vice-versa. It's ok, Dad. I know a complete sentence. I'm not an idiot. Just angry."

When I finished writing that day, I was exhausted but energized. How can you be both? I don't know how else to describe it. Maybe it's that feeling you get when you finally throw up from a queasy stomach. It feels so bad but so good.

The Unresolved Mandala

When I finished writing that day, I went to the computer to create a mandala from a photo I had shot of a baby grand piano.

My father had trained as a concert pianist before he turned to engineering as a career. I often went to sleep to Bach, Tchaikovsky or Beethoven coming from the living room. In fact, my across-the-street neighbors told me that in the summertime, when the windows were open, they liked to sit out on their lawn and listen to the concert coming from across the street.

We were taken to many concerts growing up. I remember all of us—Mom, Dad, and the five children who were still at home—going to a concert of a young pianist. The man had no more than gotten started, was maybe halfway through the first piece, when my father got up and said, "I can play better than this," and stormed out with all of us following him like baby ducks. I think it was the first time I realized how accomplished a musician my father was. Then, I was proud. Today I cringe at the memory.

Yes, he was accomplished, but experts can rarely teach beginners. Things get too automatic. They forget the steps of learning. So, while he instilled a love of music in all of us—maybe simply through lots of exposure—I, for one, didn't make it far in music. My early attempts at violin lasted about three years until I froze at a recital with my father accompanying me. I froze and had to take my seat. No one spoke to me. Not to scold me. Not to reassure me. No words were ever spoken. No one touched me. I had shamed the family.

To make the first mandala, I shot the piano keyboard. Then I distorted the keys because the whole music thing was distorted in my head. I loved classical music. I admired my father for his accomplishment in music. I resented him for being so critical of our early efforts to play. I still wish I could play a musical instrument. I love all kinds of music: classical, rock, country, jazz. My father hated rock and would blow up if he caught me listening to such trash on the radio.

I didn't think all these things out when I shot the keyboard and created the mandala. It just happened.

I shot the keyboard.

Then I distorted it.

Then I created the mandala.

But I didn't "resolve" it, as they'd say if it was a musical composition. I left with a feeling of dissonance, disharmony. One piece was dangling and dimmer than the others—a message to me that things would never fall neatly in place. There were things I would never make sense of. In my intellectual approach, I kept trying to put all the pieces in place. I kept trying to understand on a logical, head level. I think this mandala was my first conscious acknowledgement that I would never line up the facts and the events neatly like keys on a baby grand.

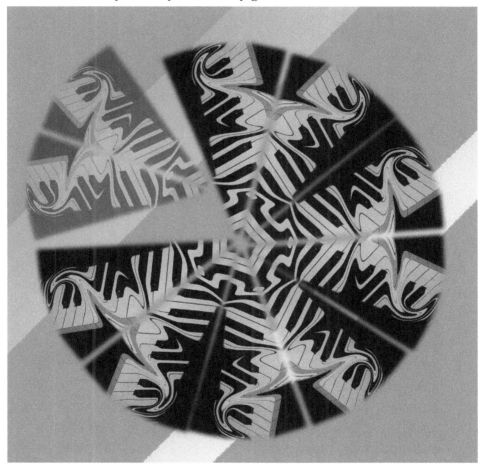

Day 2 Writing

Again, I didn't want to write. I wondered what else there was to say. But I trusted Elaine and had agreed to the assignment. I also knew I had wasted so much time on this, on him, for him, because of him, and I was determined not to waste any more. I wanted him out of my head and out of my cells. I was tired of disappearing into my turtle shell every time something brought up my fear of him.

On the second day, the pain was in my mid-back. I learned I wasn't finished with my purging. I called my father "sadistic," a strong word. I wondered about his childhood. I wondered what happened to make him kill the spirits of his children. I was really into strong language that day, using words like callous, cruel, killing, brutal.

I took up the topic of money, a bone of contention around our house. My mother was given an allowance for groceries and managed to save a little extra for unplanned expenses. She went years without new clothes. We were given a weekly allowance to cover school lunches and all incidentals, but it came with this "unworthiness" game. Every Sunday evening, when we asked for our allowance, he grudgingly gave it after asking if we thought we were worth it. It was a repetitive message played week after week, and he made it clear we better not ask for a penny more.

It taught me to be frugal. In high school, I made nearly all my own clothes and got very good at finding material on remnant tables. One time I found some pretty gold fabric and made a party dress for a school dance. The whole thing cost me $2.50. I was so proud of myself. With my long blonde hair piled high on my head, dressed in my new shimmery dress, I was a knock-out for sure and knew my father would be amazed and proud. "Dad, how do you like my dress?" I asked as I turned so he could admire all sides. "I made it for $2.50!" He was quiet just for a moment and then said, "Well, it looks like a gunny sack."

Pow. If he had hit me in the stomach, it couldn't have hurt more. My eyes almost betrayed me, but I was saved by my boyfriend knocking at the front door.

But you see? He was only telling the truth, being honest with his thoughts because he didn't know how to do anything else. He didn't know how to gauge his effect on people around him. He could do something like that and be utterly perplexed that he had stepped on anybody's party shoes. It was my fault for asking. "If you didn't want to know, why did you ask?" He didn't understand the fishing-for-a-compliment idea. He couldn't put himself in the high heels of a teenage daughter who craved a compliment from a father. Stupid me. I had this vein of optimism that one day he would look at me and say, "Wow, what a beautiful daughter I have." "Wow! What a smart, capable kid I have." "Wow!"

If he had a chance to defend himself, I think he would say, "You were so damn sensitive. Didn't you know I was teasing?" I played out this scenario in my head, imagining him saying that to me. In my imagination he was sitting at the dining room table. I stood on the opposite side and told him to be quiet and listen to me. To hear ME. The next words out of my pen were strong, capital-letter words. It had all piled up. The constant feelings of unworthiness. The scrimping for even basic stuff when we could have afforded it, and his total lack of empathy. I had gotten to a new level of anger in which this good little girl cursed the father she had been taught to honor at all costs.

DAMN IT TO HELL! I WAS SENSITIVE AND YOU KNEW IT AND PERSISTED IN "TEASING" ME. ISN'T IT SADISTIC TO DELIBERATELY DO THE VERY THING YOU KNOW WILL HURT A KID AND THEN BLAME THE KID? YOU TELL ME.

Angry words and thoughts could never be said while he was alive. I would only have been shamed one more time for being so silly, so sensitive. It was my character flaw to get over. But maybe I learned it from him. He could get hurt so easily, get angry, and stomp out of the room. Dump and run. HIS interpretation. HIS point of view. *HE WAS NEVER WRONG.* Did "I'm sorry" ever cross his lips?

On Day 2, I wrote and wrote, realizing how I kept searching for something that never seemed to happen. What confusing feelings and thoughts. I hated my father, feared him, didn't want to hurt him, and longed for his attention all at the same time. Over time, I had built walls around myself. I found safe ways to be at home and not be present. I hid in the open, aloof and withdrawn. And on Day 2, the anger spilled out. I was angrier than I had ever been with him, or with anyone, for that matter. In my head, he sat at the dining room table and didn't say a word because I wouldn't let him.

The Chaos Mandala

I was angry and upset after the second day of writing. When I went to the computer to create a mandala, I again chose an image of the baby grand piano. Since I was trying to figure out my father's psyche, I moved from the keyboard to the inside workings of the piano, the hidden parts, the cast iron frame and strings. Somehow it seemed fitting.

Mandalas are geometrical, symmetrical. Their repeating patterns are soothing and mesmerizing. The process of creating a mandala is soothing. I sit at the computer, often with classical music playing in the background. I select an image, figure out what part of the image I want to emphasize, and then go through the steps to create the mandala. The steps involve "cutting" a triangle from the picture, then copying and mirroring the triangle, and repeating the process until I have a perfect, symmetrical pattern that surprises and intrigues me. It's a meditative process. The steps slow me down, pull me out of the mood itself into the rhythm of copying, pasting, mirroring, twirling. I focus on the steps, not the mood, and wait for the gift that appears in the completed mandala. Even when the mood is negative and dark, the process and the intrigue of each step drain the toxicity from my blood.

But this time was different. I chose the image, cut the triangle using a random degree for the angle. In my anger and my haste, I didn't think it through. I know the degrees that result in equal sections when you cut a circle. Only numbers that divide equally into 360 will work. The angle I used didn't work.

Chaos. That's what I saw when I tried to resolve the pattern. The mandala was anything but soothing, mesmerizing, and satisfying. It was just the opposite. I saw scary, screaming faces, two of them whole and a third split in half. Parts of the pattern were fuzzy, parts in sharp focus. In two of the sections, the strings formed right angles. One section of strings didn't have a mirrored partner. The pieces were put together sloppily, as if someone was in a hurry—or angry.

Although it was not a soothing experience, it didn't matter. The mandala said exactly what I was feeling. Unresolved patterns. My mind was letting go of order and logic and sense-making. It felt dark and chaotic, like I was losing control. Indeed, I was losing control over the control I had kept on the emotions and feelings in the deepest part of my heart.

I didn't come away from that session of writing and mandala-making with any sense of having made progress. I had reached a new level of anger, listened to myself, spoken feelings to the father in my head. But I didn't, that day, realize the importance of what had happened. This was the beginning of the letting go— the day I couldn't resolve the pattern.

Logically, I could say to myself, and probably had a hundred times, *There are things you will never understand.* But I always believed otherwise. I always thought if I tried harder, learned a little more psychology, had a few more facts, it would all make sense. I don't know how the mandala got into places words hadn't. I couldn't resolve the pattern, and the faces were crying to me that I would *NEVER* resolve the pattern. I heard them crying: *Let it go, let it go.*

Day 3 Writing

When I sat down to write on the third day, I found out that someone had left the door to ANGER wide open. Someone had been carefully guarding that heavy door for a long time, but she up and cracked it open and then forgot to close and lock it.

I wasn't finished with what I had started the day before. In fact, I had just gotten started. My father's tactic was to dump and run. Explode. Rage. Stomp out of the room without giving anyone a chance to rebut or defend or even respond. On Day 3, in my anger, I described his tantrums as "napalming" little children. I was really angry. Maybe even as angry as I had seen him get when I was a child. This time I was the one on the exploding end rather than the receiving end.

My arm hurt from my angry words. I might as well have been lifting weights, doing curls. My forearm felt like a rock. Pains were shooting through my ear; my throat was scratchy and begging to become sore. My back hurt. Writing about him brought back all this tension in my body. But I continued to write, telling my father in my head that he couldn't storm out of the room this time. I told him to sit there and listen until I spilled my guts into his lap. I told him to sit there until I vomited everything and smeared it all over his face until he cried for mercy. This was my four-year-old speaking! She's quite imaginative, and she had been holding back for a long, long time. I didn't know she was capable of such words and such thoughts.

I was his first daughter, named for him. Maybe it was appropriate to use his own tactics against him. Even so, a part of me—that damn logical brain—was saying, "Whoa. Let's look for some balance here. There were the good things, the good genes, the college education."

"Granted. Now shut up," I said to Miss Logic. "This is *anger* speaking—the voice that was never, never, never allowed to speak. This is the sensitive side that was told to not be so sensitive, to quit crying. Well, the crying is shut up. This is cold, hard anger for all the ways he belittled his children and his wife."

You see? It was someone else's turn to speak. My logical brain had hogged the stage all my life. I could list all the defenses I had given him: only child with an overprotective mother; best teenage friend committed murder; loss of first wife to cancer; WWII; many children; stressful job. He pushed his feelings into a closet and closed the door, never to be spoken about again. He was busy doing important things, and we were, after all, just children.

I had tried over and over, for years upon years, to figure it out logically. It hadn't worked. I, too, had learned to stuff it into a closet and close the door. I, too, had learned to stay busy doing important things to avoid whatever it was I was trying to avoid. I was at last finished with trying to give him the benefit of the doubt. That's what this writing brought me to. That's what the Day 2 mandala convinced me of. I screamed in my head. The anger exploded. I couldn't stop it. I didn't want to stop it. Because he could not deal with his feelings, his loss, his grief, his disappointments, he took it out on his family.

No more. I was going to do whatever it took to get the poison out of my head, the muck out of my belly, and if that meant being four-year-old angry about it, that's what I would do. This was the "I hate you" stage. And I truly, at that moment, hated him. So, I said to the "poor man" in my head, "Sit at this table and eat my vomit just like you used to make me gag on turnips."

Yes, this was my four-year-old standing up for me. My one little act of rebellion growing up was to refuse to eat turnips because they made me gag. That's a pitiful act of rebellion. Really pitiful. I wish I could come up with something better. Breaking a family treasure. Running away from home. Getting drunk at my high school prom. But no, that was it. I wouldn't eat turnips. I was too terrified to even be in the vicinity of anyone doing anything wrong. I was good girl times ten. I just wouldn't eat turnips. Didn't he understand that I felt like I would throw up all over the table? I ate everything else. Was it too much to ask to be excused from turnips?

The next thing I wanted to vomit was the big family secret. I was eighteen when I was told about my father's first wife. I was thirty-five when I finally got up the nerve to ask why he didn't tell us about her and why I was never told that my two oldest brothers had a different mother. I wanted an explanation, a reason. It didn't come. Instead, I was told, "Everyone else figured it out. We thought you would, too." Well, shut my mouth. I was stupid, wasn't I? No, I didn't figure it out. I never even suspected. Why should I? My parents were so nitpicky about correct facts, correct pronunciation, proper grammar, honesty. Why would I even suspect they could lie about something so big?

"Well, it wasn't really a lie," I hear a brother say. "Not technically."

That's the way it was in my family. Intellectuals can split hairs on technicalities. I wasn't that smart. I was gullible and thought more in generalities. A lie, to me, could just as easily be something not said as something that was. The "lie," the "overlooked fact," the "secret"—whatever it was—made something break in me. The night I learned about Wife-and-Mother #1, I cried into my pillow for a long, long time. I remember my intellectual brain asking why I was crying. *It happened so long ago*, I reasoned. *They're all over it. Why does it matter?* I couldn't figure out why I was crying, as hard as I tried. My pillow was wet, and the tears were coming from somewhere deep inside. I had no language to answer my own question. Was I crying for a woman who died and left two little boys behind? Was I crying for my father? Why was I crying? I didn't know.

At thirty-five, when I finally asked the "why weren't we told" question, I was reminded that I must have fallen off a turnip truck. Well, they didn't exactly say "turnip truck." They had given up on turnips. But everyone else had figured it out, just not the eldest daughter who never made straight As anyway. What would you expect from her? Grow up, they said.

"Oh yeah?" I said to my dead father who was still sitting at the table in my head because I wouldn't let him leave until I had thrown up ALL the turnips. "Oh yeah?" My four-year-old stomped her foot for emphasis. "When are YOU going to figure it out? I'm not afraid of you anymore. So, grow up yourself."

From the time I was told that everyone had figured it out, it would be another eight years and my father would be dying before he at last said, "You think we weren't very nice for not telling you about Jane. I would like to tell you about her." It was a bittersweet story, and she sounded like someone I would have liked to have known. And I cried again.

The Anger Mandala

Thinking my four-year-old thoughts and feeling her anger, my thirty-five-year-old thoughts and her anger, my sixty-plus-year-old feelings and her anger, I wanted to hit something, throw something, break something. After writing, I went to the computer once again to try to make something symbolic from a feeling.

What does anger look like?

It's red. Fiery red.

That's all I knew when I started searching for a photograph. Although I had seen anger before, I had never felt it so deeply within myself. But I knew I'd recognize the right picture when I saw it.

I found what I was looking for in a bromeliad. Bromeliads grow in tropical climates and rain forests, and, according to a description, they "can adapt to the unfavorable growing conditions that exist in most homes." Hmm. I had photographed this bromeliad in the high dessert. It had a deep red center for collecting rain. Bold red, green and white spiky leaves place the plant in the "very strong statement" category. I wouldn't have to do a lot of work.

In Photoshop, I cut a triangle from the photograph. Copied it. Mirrored it. Rotated it. My breathing slowed and became deeper. I focused on the process of creating a mandala and lost track of time. Once again, I was calmed by the process and surprised by the result. In the mandala, I saw an explosion of blood-red flames shooting out in four directions. I saw eight bubble teardrops forming a protective wall around a dark center. When I looked carefully at the center, I could hardly believe my eyes. There was a square package, a box tied tightly with cords. There in the heart of the mandala, and in my own heart, safely locked away, were the feelings, emotions, family secrets, betrayals, grief, and all of life that had been too hard to handle. It was all there in the mandala. I didn't plan it. I couldn't have. But it's all there: the feelings held tightly inside, the cups of tears circling the wrapped box and the exploding temper and anger.

Yes, Elaine, Day 3 was tough.

Day 4 Writing

Something was very different when I woke up on the fourth day. I felt different. I remember asking myself, "Where am I?" Not where physically, but where inside. I went through a question-and-answer conversation with myself. "Is this forgiveness?" I asked. "No, it's not forgiveness," I answered. "Then what is it?" "Acceptance," said the inner teacher.

The dread of writing was gone. I was actually anxious to write again. I wanted to know what came next.

"Maybe he did love us," I wrote. "In his own way." But he never seemed to notice the consequences of his temper, his rage, his little "teaching moments." My mind started, once again, listing the evidence from MY point of view even as I wrote that he could only see from HIS point of view. Perspective is a hard thing to change, even at a point when we think we are at "acceptance." I had believed one thing for so long, and now it was shifting, and some part of me wanted to convince myself to hang on to the reasons for resentment.

Growing up, my reality was that I lived in a house ruled by a tyrant. I learned to tiptoe across land mines and stay out of the way. I learned to keep everything to myself, my opinions, my questions, my emotions. Up until the morning I woke up at "acceptance," I kept trying to find logical reasons to help me make this man something I longed for and something he never was—a loving father "who cared about his children's welfare."

But even as I wrote those words, I knew that wasn't correct. Someone who doesn't care about your welfare doesn't send you to college or even to the dentist. He did both. I just wanted something he didn't know how to give. I wanted to know that I was a real person who mattered for who and what I was, not a project to be worked on until I was something I was not.

But now it was time to accept reality, to quit thinking reality would be anything different if only I could put the pieces together in a way that made sense. Did he ever get to that point in his life? Did he ever look at the wake of damage he left in his path? He was stuck in my head as a big, bad ogre, and I had grown comfortable with that. *Why should I change? Did he ever change? Did he, huh?* In my myopic vision, I would give him no slack, no benefit of the doubt, no possibility of changing or being anything different than my long-held idea of him. My mind was looking for any straw to clutch so I could stay comfortable in my angst. *Nanny, nanny, boo-boo. If he never changed, why should I?* Whatever he could do, I could do better. Talk about a role model. Good grief am I stubborn.

My stubborn self still wanted some things explained. My four-year-old came out to say, "Why didn't we ever celebrate?" My list-maker chimed in with reasons many families would have celebrated: "Brother did this, check; sister did that, check; I did that other, check; brother . . ." and on and on. My sarcastic storyteller said, "Forget it. It was just another day in the life of Ivan the Terrible. Not quite good enough. But, okay, congratulations. Please pass the turnips."

Reality: I lived with a man who terrorized his family with an uncontrollable rage. Though I had moved away long ago, I kept trying to rewrite the story with a fairy-tale ending. Spending hours and journals and years trying to figure it out is not exactly accepting reality. But it did assure me in my line of defense, my line of excuses for not looking at my own wake of—yikes— destruction.

There on Day 4, the chink in the wall allowed something to sneak past the guards and whisper something about the share of people I had hurt by living in a wish world and spending so much time in the past. I was beginning to see it was me who had to let go of the contents of locked chests. Maybe my dad did live in the past, holding his secrets and hurts closely guarded. He taught me well. I was his first daughter. He was my role model.

It's hard to look out from hurt and see that others are hurting as well. No one escapes pain, and no one deserves it any more or less than anyone else. But we all experience hurt. It's part of being human. It's how we grow. He used to quote Mark Twain, saying, "People are just about as happy as they make up their minds to be." Maybe he was trying to remind himself. Or maybe he believed it and was trying to tell me to do the same.

Even though I woke up thinking I was at acceptance, there was one last thing to say to the man seated at the table in my head, and I had to say it loud enough so I, myself, could hear it. I declared my independence: "The wreckage of your eldest daughter stops here and now. You were what you were, and all the wishing and longing and grieving and trying to understand will never change who you were. You were Hurricane Katrina, and the dam no longer holds water. You used to call me Katrina, remember? Was that prophetic? Well, my dam has burst, and it's about damn time."

The damn dam WAS broken, and it WAS about time. My father was an engineer who knew about building dams and bridges. This one was mine, however, and I had to fire him as the sidewalk superintendent I kept looking to for acceptance. My accepting reality meant realizing that I could not, in reality, look to him for acceptance and approval. That's a lot of accepting and realities to put in one sentence, but probably not enough for one lifetime.

My father was who he was because of his hurts, his life events. He could look at world events objectively, and he remained fascinated with politics and world affairs up to the day he died. He appreciated other cultures. He read good books. But some things eluded him. He couldn't relate to his family. (Oops. It happened again. I slipped into that awful habit of speaking for others and not just for myself.) I will rephrase. We—he and I—never made it to an honest, caring relationship. I never saw him interacting with others in the family in a way that would make me think it was different for my brothers and sisters. But then, I wasn't around all the time. I was around as little as possible. It was what I did for self-preservation. So, I can't speak for anyone but myself.

I was teetering towards acceptance, but a part of me just wouldn't let go. There were still some things I had to say out loud, my pen talking to my paper. Until I acknowledged how deeply I felt some stuff, I was still lying to myself. Until my little four-year-old felt heard, really heard, she couldn't let go. It was she who got stuck way back there in "Who can I trust?" I was still playing a wishful-thinking game for her, a poor-me game, an "ain't it a shame" game. I had never, in my entire life, let myself feel the anger. I had, just as I had been taught, pushed it into a box, wrapped it with strong cord, and shoved it in the closet. Little kids simply do not speak that way about their parents. And besides, I was determined never to lose control of my emotions— my anger and rage—like he had. I was determined to be a better person than I perceived him to be. To me, rule number one for being a better person was "Never lose your temper under any circumstance." But never losing your temper means denying your anger, even when anger is the most appropriate of responses.

My pen went on talking, giving it one last shot. I thought about this and that and realized I could go through the list of grievances one more time. But no. I was through. It was finished. The game was over. I would quit blaming him. I would let him go. "You are excused. You may leave the table."

And as he stood to go, I realized he helped make me who I am.

And I was beginning to know and like me.

The Acceptance Mandala

Once again, after writing, I went to the computer to create a mandala to capture my feelings. I chose an image of a rose taken in Santa Fe during the celebration of my mother's life. A beautiful rose with thorns and morning dewdrops, red, her favorite color. The mandala unfolded quietly. Tears shone like luminescent pearls. The thorns in the center grew together to form protective arms. The eight spokes reached out to form calliope pipes or flutes—musical, lyrical, harmonious, peaceful. "Two things pierce the human heart," said Simone Weil. "Beauty and affliction." My heart was pierced.

I looked at the anger and acceptance mandalas side by side. Same colors. Similar shades of red and green. Where anger had a dark center with a box wrapped up tight, acceptance had a light center with musical instruments reaching out. The red in anger exploded and overpowered. The red in acceptance unfolded gracefully, carrying little pearls of wisdom in its petals.

Then I saw it.

There in the anger mandala. Another shape, another symbol: four little hearts, disguised and overshadowed by the strong red rays bursting out. The tiny hearts touched my own heart at a deeper level than anything I had written. A thunderbolt struck me, and I sat stunned in quiet wonder.

Hearts. There, in the midst of the red anger explosion. It was then that I knew, without a shadow of a doubt, that my father, in his own way, wanted to love us, *DID* love us. His own brokenness and his rage overshadowed his attempts to reach us. I cried new tears from a new place. I am sorry I never knew the real man who was my father.

A Word about Grief

Many years later, I was journaling about grief, what it is and what it does to us. I was drawn to Henri Nouwen's *The Inner Voice of Love: A Journey through Anguish to Freedom*. Nouwen says:

There is a deep hole in your being, like an abyss. You will never succeed in filling that hole, because your needs are inexhaustible. You have to work around it so that gradually the abyss closes. Since the hole is so enormous and your anguish so deep, you will always be tempted to flee from it. There are two extremes to avoid: being completely absorbed in your pain and being distracted by so many things that you stay far away from the wound you want to heal.

I have taken both paths—absorbed one moment, total avoidance the next. Reading Nouwen's extremes, I knew I wasn't alone. He named my pain as well as my defense mechanisms. Staying so busy I didn't have time to think, I would exhaust myself with activity and commitments. And then, exhausted or between commitments, I would go down that dark well. My choice was fleeing or darkness. There was a deep hole I couldn't seem to fill no matter how hard I tried.

The particular four-day write and mandala-making I've described was followed by several more equally revealing assignments. Elaine and James Pennebaker understood the pain beneath defense mechanisms and led me forward with several more four-day writes. Carl Jung reached out across the years and, from another dimension, gave me an art form that symbolically spoke in ways that words alone could not. All together, we broke through a lifelong stuck place, and I am more grateful than I will ever be able to put in words.

Since that time, I have used four-day writes and creating related mandalas to help me work through other issues and emotions. They're heavy, they're hard, they're emotional, and they are so very helpful for deep work.

Summary: Four-Day Writes

Four-day writes can be used for almost any issue you want to understand at a deeper level. However, we develop defense mechanisms for good reasons, and changing them is hard work. Do not hesitate to look to professional help, particularly if the issue you want to address includes trauma of any kind. A good therapist is worth her/his weight in gold.

Find time when you can write for four days in a row.

Go to a quiet place where you will not be interrupted.

Write fast without stopping for at least twenty minutes.

Write without editing or censoring. Let whatever words come come.

Write for your eyes only. No one needs to see what you wrote.

Allow some recovery time. Don't squeeze your writing into a busy schedule where you have to rush off immediately afterwards.

NOTE: For more in-depth information on writing about deep issues and traumas, please refer to *Opening Up: The Healing Power of Expressing Emotions* by James W. Pennebaker, PhD.

Summary: Photo Mandalas

Creating photo mandalas as I have described requires an understanding of Photoshop. There are several computer programs that will create mandala designs from your photographs. The results are instantaneous and magical. For me, the slower process of cutting a triangle, mirroring and twirling, and being able to watch and anticipate the design as it develops is core to the calming nature of the work.

- Go with your instinct. Don't analyze or pre-think why you choose a particular photo.
- Don't rush the process. Take your time.

- Carefully line up the pieces so they are perfect mirror images.
- Have soft music playing in the background if it helps you relax.
- When the mandala is done, sit quietly and allow the image to speak to you.
- Go back to it the next day or the next week and see if you see something new.

For more information, see Part 3: How to Create Mandalas.

I have a little shadow that goes in and out with me, And what
can be the use of him is more than I can see.
Robert Louis Stevenson, "My Shadow"

CHAPTER 3: SHADOWS AND ARCHETYPES

I have several little shadows that go in and out with me. At one time, a long time ago, I thought I was perfect, or at least tried hard to be perfect. And when I wasn't, I had good reasons and could defend myself and my actions. Rationalization was not a conscious word in my vocabulary, but it was certainly alive and well in my life.

I couldn't see the shadows in myself until someone introduced me to them. It was a simple enough exercise, innocent on the surface. It's a good place to start.

The Good, the Bad and the Ugly — Part 1

Name ten people you admire. They can be friends or famous, living or dead. List them in your journal. Describe them.

Who are they?

What traits do you admire in them?

What draws you to them?

Be as specific as you can and as expansive as you can. Write it in paragraphs or put it in a table with names in one column and traits in the second. Take your time to think about each one of them. Maybe even be grateful for who they are, what they represent to you, and how they inspire you.

Now, here's the cool part: *The very traits you identify are also in you!*

Wow! That is beyond-belief amazing! I have things in common with Brené Brown, Meryl Streep, Naomi Shihab Nye, Michelle Obama, and my best friends whom I love dearly! As I write about these people in my journal, I realize how exceptional each one is. They are all strong women.

Insightful. Caring. Communicators. Sexy. Humorous. Sincere. Dang! I'm feeling pretty good about myself! I'm in real good company!

Bask in part one for a day or two. Enjoy it! Then, when you're ready, do the second part of this exercise.

The Good, the Bad and the Ugly — Part 2

Name ten people who get under your skin, people who hook you, make you extremely angry, livid even. Do this in a table form. Don't write and write about them. Just identify the traits that make you so mad you can't see straight. What is it about each one that hooks you? Be as specific as possible.

Well, guess what? You know what's coming, and I'm sorry. Those same unfavorable traits you identified are often the very shadows you don't want to acknowledge in yourself. *NO! NO! NO! Absolutely not!*

The first time I did this exercise, I was mad all day long. I named that person who always has to be right, always has to have the worst ain't-it-awful story. ("You think that's bad, wait 'til you hear what happened to me!") That person always gets under my skin. Don't even get me started. And don't you dare tell me that I'm that way!

Since I am mostly a rule follower and since I started the exercise, I had to finish it. Besides, I had heard this ugly idea in too many places from too many faces to ignore. It was shadow work. Few of us enjoy doing shadow work. I had to write out my anger, my denial, my liar-liar-pants-on-fire retort until a crack opened in my façade. *Okay then, maybe I'm a tiny bit like that person in certain circumstances. Maybe an itsy-bitsy-teeny bit, but I'm nowhere near as bad as she is! Or he is! Or they are! Why am I getting so upset and defensive? What is it I don't want to see about myself?*

Perhaps because I was such a perfectionist, a rule follower, a fit-in-at-all-costs kind of person, I could not see my own quirks, faults, shadows. It took a lot of writing and soul-searching to even glimpse those shadows. Owning them was even harder. (*Really, I've got good reasons when I act that way. Let me explain!*) After many pages of ink, and denial, and finally a bit of acceptance, this has become a regular go-to in my toolbox. Often, I don't write about it. I just notice. When someone hooks me and I feel my defenses coming forward to protect me, I stop and wonder how I am like this person who is rubbing me so wrong. What do I not want to see in myself?

I used to think I had all the answers, the logical, *it-makes-perfect-sense* answers. Why couldn't people see the messes they were in, the obvious choices they could make? To me, it was as plain as the noses on their faces. It took doing this exercise over and over and over for me to see my shadows peeking around the corner. Like many perfectionists, I'm an expert at denial—perfect, in fact. I had not learned to recognize and accept the bads and the uglies in me along with the goods.

Remember that spiral way of learning? This is a good example. I had to revisit this idea over and over before it sunk in. I didn't want it to be true. But once I got over my defensiveness, I could see a glimmer of truth in *hook = shadow*. That doesn't mean it was easy; nor was it over. People continue to hook me, and I continue to meet my shadows in those hooks.

Another hard part of this exercise for me is that once I have an *Aha!* about myself, I go back and review my entire life from the new perspective. Things I was so sure about take on a whole different slant. Who I thought I was wasn't totally who I was. Like that time I was so adamant I was right, and now I see I was so wrong. It is quite humbling to realize I was wrong, wrong, wrong, dead wrong. (Okay, that's a bit harsh. I've been there many times—beating myself up for not knowing something before I learned it.)

Regret is a heaviness in the heart and soul, and when it gets too heavy, please call in the helpers. I did the best I could with the information and understanding I had at the time. We all do. Now I am older, wiser, and humbled. Definitely older, definitely humbled, hopefully wiser. We need to look back with compassionate eyes, not only on other people, but also on our younger selves.

Perfectionism can be hard on a body. I can beat myself up most thoroughly. Next year, I'll undoubtedly look back at something I said or did today and shake my head. The point is to keep learning and to become more accepting of others *and* of yourself.

Be Compassionate with Yourself

Take the time to find your shadows, but do it compassionately. Be kind to yourself. Spend equal time on the good stuff, the people you admire. This exercise isn't just to uncover the dark shadows, the so-called garbage. It's also to own the good stuff you may not have realized is YOU. And, by the way, this "garbage" is more like compost, and compost always helps our gardens grow. I would not be who I am today without all the lessons, challenges, mistakes and stumbles—the compost that helped me grow. I would not be who I am without the encouragement, inspiration, and acceptance as well.

Talking to the Shadow People

I have found that I need to go beyond "How am I like this person?" to a deeper level of understanding. I use a dialogue or interview method of journaling to get to know my shadow people. I personify them. Talk to them. Interview them. Sometimes even name them.

Take *depression*, for example. While I have never experienced clinical depression and don't want to make light of it, I have had days, weeks, and even months of being down a deep, dark well. I have, more than once, been on antidepressants. I'll call my visitor *depression* with a small *d*. Not the capital-*D Depression*. Maybe Mr. Blues. He's real and has come to visit every now and then. I saw him one day, sitting quietly in a dark corner, a presence just beyond my consciousness until I felt him in the room. He was dressed in dirty, tattered clothes, a homeless person hunched over, sad, withdrawn, patiently waiting for my attention.

"Why are you here?" I asked him.

He began to speak slowly and quietly so I had to lean forward to hear. I had to go sit beside him to hear his words. This time, instead of shooing him away, I let him talk as long as he wanted. I asked questions to make sure I understood what he was saying to me. We talked back and forth for several pages. Finally, when I felt I had heard him, and felt him, and understood what he was trying to tell me, we sat silent for a while side by side. Then I gently thanked him for his insights and politely asked him to leave.

It would not have been productive to ignore him when I saw him sitting there. He has a way of sticking around if I do that. His earlier tactic was to trip me and send me flying headfirst down the dark well, especially when I kept a busy schedule specifically to keep him away. Over time I've learned that if I turn to him, sit beside him, let him talk, be with him a while, he will give me his message and then leave when I ask him to. Maybe he'll stay for the day. But he doesn't move in, take up residence, outstay his welcome. He has become a messenger, warning me or pulling back a curtain to show me something I need to see.

Other shadows have been similar for me. Once I identify them and give them my full attention for a bit, they seem to lose their grip. Like Mr. Blues, they can be messengers. My wicked witch, Hildegard, may not come often, but when she does, it's in a flash. She takes over my speech and my usual calm demeanor. She stuns everyone around, including me.

My Wicked Witch Came Out Last Night.
Who is she—this me I deny?
She holds on to old tattered garments,
Puts them on and flaunts them.
She stirs old pots, old messes, cobwebs of places lived
    long ago.
She chokes me with the dust of memories and patterns I
    had safely stored.
What does she want to tell me as she magnifies the slights
    and sights of scowls?
She destroys my illusions with illusions of her own.
What purpose does she serve me?
Last night I let her speak.
I didn't stuff her in the farthest reaches of my mind.
She's a shadow of something unspoken and tangled.
Her dagger is mistrust.
Eyes vigilant and cold,
Mouth narrow and set,
She will not listen to reason.
She knows the wounds that bleed and pricks them open
    over and over and over.
When her blood lust is satisfied, she simply vanishes in
    a puff of smoke,
Leaving me to stare at the ashes
and look for a broom.

Until we accept our shadows, acknowledge them, know them for who they are, they will stay underground and sabotage us in ways we don't understand, in ways that hurt who we want to be, and in ways that hurt the very relationships we cherish. Hildegard has done that a few times. I apologize. And I hear her cackling that my inner work is not done.

Sometimes I'll glimpse a shadow and not know who it is. A feeling, an uncertainty, an inkling. The following is an example of an underground shadow that tripped me up so many times my nose should have been broken; it was certainly out of joint often enough. It's another example of how writing and creating mandalas helped me grasp what I could not see with my logical brain alone.

Grief Revisited

It was about a year after my work with Elaine. I thought I was safe, through it all, moved on. But one day *anger* hit me upside the head with a baseball bat. At least, I thought it was anger. He was dressed in the clothes of anger and walked with the stance of anger. Only after I felt my blood boil did he remove his outer layer of clothes to reveal rags and tatters and utter despair, and finally, grief.

It doesn't matter what opened the door. That door was bound to open sooner or later. This time it was a simple little incident with all the layers and complexities of simple little incidents. A significant someone—okay, it was my husband—was blaming someone else for something he should have done himself. He hadn't asked questions, hadn't prepared for this twelve-mile hike we were on. He was blaming the woman at the rental place because he had rented only one hiking pole instead of two, and *SHE should have known he'd need two* for this rocky, steep part of the trail. He was frustrated about the precariousness of the path, but frankly, I was tired of people blaming others for their own decisions.

You idiot, I thought. *It was not her fault. Why didn't* YOU *think about these things? Why didn't* YOU *spend the time to prepare?* I didn't say it out loud—only in my head. I fell back into my childhood pattern of withdrawing. But I was angry enough to stay silent and fuming, and to close the curtains of my eyes so he would see only dark clouds and thunderstorms if he looked. But he was too busy navigating the rocks to even notice. Since we were on a twelve-mile hike and there were eleven miles to go, I couldn't exactly respond in my usual way, make an excuse to go on some errand just to get out of the house. Also, I should have known that when my reaction is an overreaction to a situation, there's something more going on. We walked in silence and I thought horrible thoughts. The day wore on. We stopped for lunch. Back to the trail. Back to my horrible thoughts.

And then the light shifted in the dense forest on the mountain.

There on that long trail where I could not escape, the mirror turned and quietly whispered, *"You are not the fairest in the land."* What? *"You had choices. You didn't ask questions. You didn't do the preparation."* And I thought about all the times in my life when I had blamed other people, all my regrets for my "non-choices" when I gave other people charge over my life. This shadow had been following me around for years, and it took a simple incident, with someone I deeply cared for, to finally trip me up and make me notice.

Anger comes with a baseball bat, but grief seeps in slowly and steadily until the landscape changes. Or maybe I'm talking about the acceptance part of grief. I usually stop at anger. That's as far as I usually get before I throw up an instantaneous dam. This time, it didn't hold. There were too many cracks in the dam, too many cracks in my theories, too many cracks in my beliefs, and a big crack in a self-image I had worked so hard to guard.

It took several days for the full force of this flood to take me down. I resisted as long as I could. When I could resist no more, I understood that so much of what I believed all my life, what I based my comings and goings and doings on, was false, or at least not completely true. It was only my truth, my belief, my perspective. Now there was a big emptiness because what I thought was true was no longer true. What could fill this vacuum?

I sat in a dark place for a long time.

My analytic brain tried to take over: *Write something. Do something. Do anything. Don't just sit there.*

I had no energy to do anything but sit there and wallow.

Wallow is such a loaded, critical, unhelpful word. I have had little patience for wallowers. And here I was. Immobile. Sad. Leaky eyes. No words to describe where I was or what I was thinking or what was wrong. I wasn't thinking. I was just . . . wallowing. Drowning.

Finally, I did the only thing I knew to do. I grabbed my camera and drove to the Arboretum because it's a beautiful place. I walked and walked and walked. Angrily. With purpose but no destination. Not seeing anything. I just wanted to be out in nature surrounded by flowers, trees, green grass, rocks, water. Things that weren't trying to be anything but what they were.

I took a couple shots. Out of habit. Because I needed to. I began to look for something that would express what I was feeling, say what I couldn't put words to.

There. A row of bare crepe myrtles, undressed for winter, smooth barkless trunks, dead leaves fallen to the ground. Dark shadows. Static, unmoving, bending over the path, a canopy of spindly branches filtering the sunlight. Lines going off in so many directions. No focal point. It was just a photograph. But it seemed to grasp what I could not grasp, say what I could not say.

When I got home, I made a mandala from the photograph. When I finished and wondered what to call it, "Grief and Chaos" came to mind. It was only then that I recognized what I was feeling as grief.

Grief for choices not made.

Grief for years of wearing masks.

Grief for trying to be someone I wasn't.

Grief for not being who I was.

Grief for wasted time and wasted relationships.

And the realization that there were no do-overs. What was gone was gone. I had made my choices by not making choices, not asking questions, not doing the preparation. Messages often come to me by what hooks me in other people. That's when my mirror needs to turn and whisper, "Be still, my love. Be kind. Be compassionate. But look deeper. The shadow you see in others may also be in you."

What hooks me nails me.

That day, as I stared at the mandala, I could feel only grief. I could not move beyond this dark, lonely place of regret. But I had put a name to it.

The process of making the mandala was, as before, calming, meditative. And once again, a mandala communicated something I had overlooked. For grief, it softened the edges. It showed me patterns developing from the chaos. New patterns emerging from shadows and branches. Shadows balanced with light and intricate designs. Symbols of stars and triangles widening and pointing outward, yet all flowing all the while into the center.

It did not happen instantaneously. But naming it and seeing the emerging patterns allowed me to begin working on my understanding that night as I slept. I often go to bed with a question or a problem and wake up the next morning with an inkling, or if I'm lucky, an answer. So it was I woke the next morning with a sense of new growth. Maybe even of hope. And—what was this?—of forgiveness. This time it was me who needed forgiving. And it was me who needed to do the forgiving. And most of all, it was me who needed to step up and take charge of the rest of my life.

What is it you want to do with the rest of your life? I asked.

Here's what I'd really like to do, I answered. And I said it out loud.

Then go and do it, I said. *You don't need anyone's permission. You don't need anyone's approval. You don't need to go back to school. You don't need to get your "work" done first. This IS your work. This IS your gift. This IS your assignment.*

Okay then.

And I asked my analytic self to help my child-full-of-joy self become what she always wanted to be: an artist, a photographer, a storyteller.

But wait! I said. *I'm not good enough.*

Of course not, someone inside me answered. *No one starts out as an expert. You do what you enjoy, and you get better at it.*

And I will.

Some questions I've found useful in getting to know my shadows are

- Who are you?
- Why are you here?
- What are you afraid of? What are you trying to protect me from?
- What are you trying to teach me?

- Why now?
- Ask the questions and then wait. Be patient and wait long enough for answers.

Archetypes

I don't know where to draw a line between shadows and archetypes, and that is why I'm presenting them together. For me, they intermingle in my mind. Sometimes a shadow is an emotion, like grief in the example above. But sometimes a shadow starts out as a shadow but then becomes fleshed out, having many attributes, and, for me, it becomes an archetype. Archetypes are universal, unconscious patterns of thought. Each archetype has a set of traits we can recognize in myths, movies, literature, and human behavior across cultures and time. If someone is described as a jester, hero, caregiver, or judge, for example, we instantly understand something of that person's character.

My primary mentors and teachers for archetypes are the authors Carolyn Myss, *Sacred Contracts*, and Carol S. Pearson, *Awakening the Heroes Within*. There are many others, of course, but I especially want to give these two women credit for all their research and for teaching me through their books.

There are hundreds of archetypes, some better known than others. Most of the ones in the following table are easily recognized and described, although they also have traits we might not automatically identify. Read through the list and name someone who fits. If you can't think of someone you know, think about stories you've read or movies you've seen. Once you've done that, find yourself in the list. But again, you are not a single archetype any more than you have only one shadow. We are complex beings. Myss says everyone has twelve primary archetypes, four of whom are survival archetypes: Child, Victim, Prostitute, and Saboteur. I didn't much like hearing of those four, but I stuck with her long enough to see how they played out in my life.

ARCHETYPE	PERSON OR CHARACTER
Artist	
Addict/Workaholic	
Orphan	
Victim	
Seeker	
Mentor	
Judge	
Rebel	
Athlete	
Hero/Rescuer/Knight	
Saboteur	
Caregiver	
Fool/Jester/Clown	
Warrior	
Wounded Child	
Wizard	
Prostitute	
Gambler/Risk Taker	
Eternal Child	
Martyr	
Visionary	
Servant	

Following a procedure (and extensive descriptions) in *Sacred Contracts*, I selected my twelve archetypes and had conversations with them. Each had something to tell me about my inner self. I journaled about each one, trying to be as honest as I could. I often learned more from the ones who seemed, on the surface, more negative than positive. According to Myss, however, archetypes are not positive or negative; they are neutral. We begin to see this as we learn their qualities, but I certainly placed some of them in the positive category and some in the negative, especially when I named other people who fit the categories. But just as in shadow work, we categorize archetypes from initial reactions, impressions, and behaviors that hook us. It's human nature. We judge and categorize. But each of us is much more than a category or judgment. The very same traits, in fact, can be productive in one situation and nonproductive in another.

The characteristics of the compulsive gambler, for example, are also seen in the entrepreneur who takes risks. When *Gamblers/Risk-Takers* win big, we admire them. When they lose, we scorn them for taking unreasonable risks. It's that darn *Judge* inside, a real part of all of us!

We can be critical of our *Judges*, both when they're too hard on us and when they're so, well, judgmental of others. But they also help us discern what to do, hopefully know a scam when we see one, and not be taken in.

Victim always brings up negative vibes for me. It's been one of the hardest archetypes for me to own. Although my story is not any more dramatic than anyone else's, I've held that story precious as a get-out-of-jail-free card. I called on *Victim* for excuses as to why I had done this or that instead of taking full responsibility for my life choices.

All of us have the *Victim* archetype, according to Myss, and it's somewhat reassuring to me that I'm not alone. *Victim* might be my biggest hook. I can recognize it so easily in someone else and rationalize it so easily in myself. The positive aspect of the *Victim*, Myss says, is that it becomes the guardian of self-esteem. For me, that happens when *Victim* sends up a red flag anytime I make excuses, blame someone else for my predicament, or turn my power of choice over to someone else. That little feeling in my gut can't be blamed on indigestion.

Victim was not an easy write. My relationship to *Victim* wasn't clear in a week or a month or even a year. I've spiraled back to this archetype over and over. I've gone from total denial, to acceptance, to beating myself up for giving *Victim* so much power, to asking for help, and even to having a little more compassion for others who are in their *Victim*'s grip.

I did the same kind of scrutiny and writing for my *Wounded Child* whose core issues are dependency and abandonment; my *Saboteur* who is so afraid of change she often prevents me from moving forward; my *Eternal Child* who eternally wants to play.

I identified *Artist* as one of my archetypes even though, at that time, I didn't identify myself as an artist. Through my journaling, I realized how much I admired people who allowed themselves to play with various art mediums. I recognized my wishing and longing to get my own hands dirty. But I had thoroughly absorbed the idea that to do something you really enjoyed was selfish, particularly if others around you were working hard or needing help. (And there are ALWAYS people around who are working hard or needing help.)

Just as with *Victim*, *Artist* was not a smooth, easy or instant transformation. I traced my longing back to a time when I was freer to explore that side of me, and I, timidly at first, invited *Artist* back into my life. (Julia Cameron encouraged me, cajoled me, and gave me exercises. She'll do the same for you in her book *The Artist's Way*.)

I created a space for *Artist* in my house, and the space sat unused for a long time. Evidently it was okay to organize a space, it just wasn't yet okay to *play* in that space! Then, bit by bit, I created spaces in my schedule. I took a pottery workshop, joined a photography club, took drawing classes. Little by little *Artist* came forward, dressed in a peasant skirt and wearing bangle bracelets. I had absorbed so deeply the work-before-play commandment that it took work—and play—to redefine work and play. *Artist* has taken up more and more space in my life. She fills me with joy daily when she comes to play/work.

One of the ways I summarized my work with my archetypes was to name their positive traits and then ask them what they needed in order to become more proactive rather than reactive in my life. Following is a condensed version of lots of ink on lots of journal pages.

Archetype	Positive Traits	What do you need?
Artist	Creativity, play	Keep the Judge away!
Rebel	Always questioning convention	Honest, open conversations. Ask questions!
Prostitute	Alert to soul compromises	To walk hand in hand with Rebel
Victim	Commitment to self-empowerment	Voice, gratitude, ice cream, a walk in the woods
Eternal Child	Joy, play, enthusiasm	To wake up every morning!
Orphan Child	Reminders of why this work is important	To be seen
Addict	Perseverance, habit	Commitment to a project; NO to busyness

Judge	Discernment	Balance, a blindfold, don't bring me in too early
Mentor	Sharing, teaching	Not to take over
Seeker	Curiosity, always learning	Openness
Saboteur	Gut instinct, warning	Slow down and pay attention
Athlete	Self-discipline, focus, confidence	Regular exercise

Which archetypes describe you? Pick one or two and describe both their good qualities and their shadow sides. Think about situations in your life where a particular archetype is most evident. Have a conversation with that archetype. Start with your best, your favorite, especially if this is following a shadow exercise. But also, based on the shadow exercise, which archetypes might personify your shadow characteristics?

Some questions to ask:

- How are you an integral part of me?
- How have you contributed to my life?
- When are you most likely to come out?
- What are your positive attributes?
- What are your negative attributes?
- What do you need in order to be more proactive and less reactive in my life?

The Learning Spiral

As you write about shadows and archetypes, remember the spiral of learning. Something becomes clear and we think we know. Then something else happens and we find a deeper meaning. Again and again we spiral closer and closer to deep understanding.

Archetype work and shadow work are never done. We continue to learn. As you journal about your hidden selves, be quiet, be still, be open, and, above all, be nonjudgmental.

Allow your shadows and archetypes to show up. Listen to what they have to say even if you disagree, even if it's hard.

Parker Palmer, in *A Hidden Wholeness*, refers to a soul being like a wild animal, easily frightened back into the woods. In his Circles of Trust, we are taught how to be present, and how to listen to one another so attentively that we invite each other's souls to come forward. We sit quietly, calmly, holding our hands open. We do not judge. We simply listen. We don't think of responses or how to explain or defend or fix. We listen with our attention, our eyes, our hearts, our whole bodies. Just listen. This is what we must also do for our own shadows and archetypes to come forward. They can hide so easily behind our walls and defenses.

Summary: Shadows and Archetypes

- The traits you admire in others are also in you.
- The traits you despise in others may reveal something to you about your own shadows.
- Shadows can sabotage us unless and until we acknowledge them.
- Archetypes are neither positive nor negative.
- Talk to your shadows and archetypes.
- Ask questions. Listen for answers.
- Learning occurs in a spiral as we circle back to ideas and concepts.
- Be kind to yourself as you uncover shadows and learn about archetypes.

Part 2
Lighter and Still Nourishing

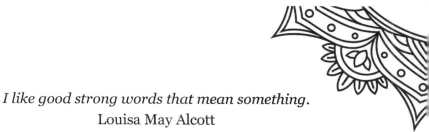

I like good strong words that mean something.
Louisa May Alcott

CHAPTER 4: USING RANDOM WORDS OR CONCEPTS AS PROMPTS

Almost all books on journaling have prompts in the form of questions. Some will open you to your thoughts and ideas. Some are the same questions you've answered since you were sixteen. (*Where do you see yourself in five years?*) In terms of the learning spiral, we have more insight at thirty-six than sixteen, and more wisdom at sixty-six than thirty-six. Thus, some of these question prompts are worth revisiting at different stages of life.

In the following exercises, rather than questions, we'll use single words or ideas presented on wisdom cards to create our own prompts. We'll play with words and concepts in a fun way that is often surprising.

The Thesaurus Game

Some friends and I once had a "Shitty First Draft Club." I wish I could take credit for that phrase, but it belongs to Anne Lamott (*Bird by Bird*). It nails what first drafts should be considered. The sooner we quit thinking we have to write perfectly from the get-go, the easier it gets to journal. And allowing ourselves to play repeatedly without censoring can lead to richer descriptions and more insightful language.

My small writing group met once a week before work. We only had forty-five minutes, a very short time period to write and share, but we were committed to trying. We designed an exercise that led to some pretty creative thinking and lots of laughter! Later, this same exercise led me to a method of creating my own prompts for my deep journaling.

We would open a thesaurus randomly, point, and move our finger to the nearest noun. After all the synonyms were read, we had five minutes to write. We were then invited to share what we had written. It was an agreed-upon rule that no one had to share. We would not even encourage (cajole, spur, push, egg on) anyone to share. It was simply an invitation.

After trying noun prompts for a while, we added adjectives, selecting both a random noun and an adjective. The two words were then used together in a five-minute write. This practice of pairing words not normally put together challenged our creativity, and often, we would find ourselves thinking about a certain combination of words throughout the day. It was like learning a new word and then seeing that word frequently and in unexpected places. But this time it was an unexpected concept, absolutely perfect to describe something in our lives or to use in a creative writing piece. (The line between journaling and creative writing can be easily blurred at times.)

While this exercise can be done on your own, it's even more fun with a few friends. Everyone brings something different to the experience; everyone has different insights. The sharing is stimulating, inspiring, and, like my SFD Club, often full of laughter! Following are a few examples of pairing random adjectives with random nouns that I put together just for this description. That's the key—*random*. Not expected. But wow! My brain has already begun working on these!

The Thesaurus Game Examples:
1. Incorrigible country
2. Short-lived transformation

3. Obsolete margin
4. Peevish dependency
5. Superficial fluff

Using Angel Cards

One morning I went to my writing room and didn't have anything to write about. I stared at an empty page and was stymied. I had no question to ask, nothing to wonder about. I had resolved some of the old issues or had let them go, knowing some would never be resolved. What in the world would I write about? I fumbled around for several days, knowing there was something to explore but not knowing what or how. I had no focus. That's when I remembered the thesaurus exercise and turned to a set of angel cards as a starting place.

Angel cards, developed by Kathy Tyler and Joy Drake, are available through your local bookstore. They are small cards with a single word on each of them, concepts like joy, love, trust, transition. Good stuff to think about. A suggested way to use the cards is to draw one each day as a sort of theme for the day. The way I used them in my journaling was to draw a random card, look up the word in the thesaurus, read all the synonyms, and start writing, just as we had in the thesaurus exercise.

When I found I wanted a little more input, I would scan my bookshelves and magically pull the right book off the shelf that would tell me something more about the concept I had drawn. How does that happen? I don't know, but it does. Time and time again!

For example, one day I drew CREATIVITY from the angel cards. A lot has been written about creativity. Personally, I have 127 books on the subject. Well, maybe not that many, but it *is* a topic I've been interested in all my life, and I do have quite a collection. But what does it mean to me? What did *I* have to say about the subject?

When I looked at my bookshelf, the book that caught my eye

was not one with creativity in the title. I have learned to trust my instinct, and so I pulled *One River, Many Wells* by Matthew Fox off the shelf. I opened the book and scanned the table of contents. Sure enough, there was a chapter on creativity. It was titled "Holy Imagination: Art and Ritual as Paths to Mindfulness." (See what I mean? It happens all the time!) In this chapter, Fox distills what Christian, Hindu, Jewish, and Muslim texts say about creativity and art. Fascinating!

From a concept on an angel card, to synonyms in a thesaurus, to a book practically falling off the shelf, I learned a lot about creativity that morning, and could be more articulate about what it means to me.

Using Wisdom Cards

While angel cards contain a single word, there are also decks of cards that contain bits of wisdom drawn from various religious or spiritual belief systems. Known as wisdom cards, oracle cards, inspirational cards, and any number of other labels, they are available from bookstores and, of course, online. I recommend the bookstores since they usually have sample decks for you to examine. Often the artwork is extraordinary, although one of my favorite decks (Pema Chödrön's Compassion Cards) has no artwork at all. I'm drawn by the artwork but choose the decks when the words speak to me or I'm intrigued by the author.

Randomly drawing a wisdom card has become a regular practice in my journaling. Drawing one in response to a question helps me imagine something from an entirely different perspective. If I stay in my own head, I can go around and around without learning anything new. If I bring in another point of view, especially from a different belief system, I'm challenged to take a good look at my own thinking.

Sometimes, like the thesaurus exercise, I draw two cards— an angel card and one from a wisdom deck, or two from two different decks. I put the concepts together and see where they lead me. I approach this exercise with a sense of curiosity and playfulness, no judgment. The value of the exercise lies in being hit with an idea entirely different from the same ideas and ruts I fall into so easily. A detour. A different path. Something I hadn't thought of. The bumping of one concept against another offers me a new way to think about something.

The Pema Chödrön cards have single sentences on the front and a longer explanation on the back. In the first month I had the cards, I randomly drew the same card three or four times—even after shuffling extensively. Crazy!

The message?

Always maintain only a joyful mind.

The message on the back went on to say, *Constantly apply cheerfulness, if for no other reason than because you are on this spiritual path. Have a sense of gratitude to everything, even difficult emotions, because of their potential to wake you up.*

Thank you, Pema. I guess I needed to hear that!

Using Mind Mapping

Another fun way to get a handle on specific concepts, and see how ideas bump up against each other, is through a brainstorming technique called mind mapping. Mind mapping has been around for centuries and has gone by various names. It's a pictorial way to show relationships among concepts or ideas.

I don't know what Leonardo da Vinci called his diagrams, but he used them extensively. (He probably never worried about calling them anything. It was just his way of thinking.) My introduction to this structured-brainstorming way of outlining came in quality circle training where the tool was called a lotus diagram. I used them to help define various research questions. The item being studied was written in the center of a grid. Surrounding that (concept, idea, problem, area of interest), I wrote all the contributing factors I could think of. Then, one by one, I would do the same with each contributing factor, naming the possible contributing factors to the contributing factor. This tool helped me get past simplistic answers to complicated questions, both in my work life and in my personal life, and became a good way to organize my thinking when I journaled.

The term *mind map* and a more free-flowing way to make the diagrams was popularized by psychologist and author Tony Buzan in a BBC TV series he hosted in the '70s. (Google *mind map* for more information. Also, check out *How to Think like Leonardo da Vinci* by Michael J. Gelb, for an excellent chapter on mind mapping.) Whatever we call them, diagrams show relationships in a way that linear outlines don't. When we realize how much everything is interrelated, it's hard to place one thing over another in a hierarchical outline.

In this example, I'm going to stay with *creativity*. Draw a circle in the middle of a blank page and write *creativity* in it. Then draw spokes leading out to other circles. Put related ideas in these circles. I used *talent, vision, genius, inspiration, resourceful*, and *clever*.

Add spokes and circles and ideas radiating out from these circles. Keep rippling out until you run dry (or reach the edge of the paper). Any one of these ideas could result in more spokes. For example, spokes from the *genius* circle might include people living or dead who I think have genius. Or take *clever*. It takes cleverness just to live life. Cleverness is fixing something using stuff you already have. One circle might just say *duct tape. Resourcefulness* is making soup out of whatever's in the refrigerator. Or making up a game on a long road trip. *Vision* might lead to *20-20, mirage, dream, insight. Talent* might lead to *musician, aptitude, practice makes perfect, artist*, or even *a unit of money.* You get the idea. No limitations. Put down anything that pops in your head. The ideas keep adding on and adding on, circles leading to circles. Connections going out and looping back in all directions. Take a look at Leonardo's diagrams sometime. There are interrelated concepts connected all over the place!

My practice is to make the mind map and add my phrases and thoughts all over the page. Sometimes I might turn to a new page and write about the concept in a usual journaling kind of way. Complete sentences and all that. But often the map has taken up all my writing time and is enough anyway. I've seen some new connections I hadn't thought of before. I may have come to some new conclusions. Whatever. It's been a fun exercise.

Summary: Thesaurus Exercise

- Gather a few friends who like to write.
- Using a thesaurus, randomly select a noun and an adjective.
- Read aloud all their synonyms.
- Put the two words together and write for five minutes.
- Share what you write (always optional).

Summary: Using Cards as Prompts

- Select cards at random and write whatever is evoked by them.
- Select cards from two different decks and write what is evoked by the ideas bumping up against each other.
- Select a card at random and look for that topic in a book on your bookshelf.
- Be open to ideas from belief systems different from your own.

Summary: Mind Mapping

- Start in the center of an unlined piece of paper.
- Draw a circle and write the concept or idea you choose as your main topic.
- Draw spokes out from the circle, leading to other circles.
- Write related concepts in these circles.
- From these secondary circles, draw spokes and circles and write related concepts or key words in them.
- Continue until you run out of paper or ideas.

NOTE: Use different colors of ink. Add sketches and images. Do whatever helps show the interrelatedness of the concepts and helps you figure out what is most important to you.

I love the way words and pictures work together on a page. I have also noticed how when wise words have visuals added to them, they seem to travel further online, like paper aeroplanes catching an updraught.
Chris Riddell, *Art Matters*

CHAPTER 5: VISUAL JOURNALING WITH COLLAGE

So, you're not an artist. So what? You *ARE* creative. Everyone is creative. It takes creativity to solve daily challenges. And you *WERE* an artist at one time. Every child who is ever born is an artist. Maybe you haven't practiced or have forgotten or were intimidated. Every child is an artist just as every child is a dancer. It's IN us until someone scares it into hiding. So there. That's my soapbox. Don't tell me you're not an artist. My hands are over my ears and I'm not listening.

Collage Journaling on Your Own

Because so many people have been intimidated by the "creativity" word, one of my favorite visual journaling methods is collage. Instead of having to draw or paint, we can tear and paste just like we did when we were in kindergarten. Select images and words from magazines, paste them into your journal and write a sentence or two. That's it! Collage journaling can be that simple.

You might select an image, imagine yourself in the image and write what you're feeling. Or you might come up with a topic first (joy, loneliness, being left out, celebration, a situation you're dealing with), skim through magazines to find an image, and then write. See a quote or even a single word in a cool font and add it to your journal.

You can, of course, get as complex as you want, and that might require additional resources. Few of us have a wide enough variety of magazines for extensive collaging. Does your local library recycle magazines? Mine has a shelf where people can leave their old magazines for others to pick up. You might find some great photos, headlines, and artwork you can use.

Collage journaling can be a valuable tool for accessing your innermost self. I suggest trying it on your own first. Then, if you want to go deeper, there are some excellent collage journaling resources out there.

Or, find a couple of friends willing to join you. But, a caution. As in any work where deep thoughts and feelings can come out, choose people you trust, and establish clear understandings. Confidentiality is critical in any kind of self-exploration work.

I have used collage-making as a get-acquainted activity in retreats. Have a variety of magazines and images on hand and ask people to create a collage that says something about themselves. With a time limit, say twenty minutes, people don't worry too much about making a perfect art piece. (Know your group, though. Even this might be too intimidating for some.)

Collage Journaling in Groups

Working in groups can bring a deep richness as we learn from each other's experiences and perspectives. I've had the good fortune of being in collage groups with two gifted and trained facilitators. One is also a Jungian psychologist. While credentials of this level are not required to facilitate collage groups, some understanding of participating in circles is important. Some basic understanding and agreement about confidentiality, sharing workspace, the tone of the gathering, etc. will go a long way towards having a satisfying and insightful experience. (See Part 3: Suggested Circle Guidelines.)

My facilitator friends, Pam and Gail, have an art studio that can accommodate a dozen people seated around tables. Along one wall are drawers and cabinets full of images collected over the years. Along another wall are bins of fabric scraps organized by color. There are trinkets of all kinds, scrapbooking papers, wallpaper sample books, a copier to reduce or enlarge images, and, of course, pots of glue, paintbrushes, colored pens, ribbons, buttons, and more. It's a paradise for collaging! We observe the following format:

Allow a full day of uninterrupted time. Dedicated time is an important factor: think time, play time, get-out-of-your-analytical-left-brain time. Sharing time is also important when we present our work to each other and are open to feedback.

Set an intention. The day begins with an opening circle in which the facilitator sets an intention. A question is asked or a prompt is given. We write for several minutes and then have the opportunity to share our responses, with sharing always being optional.

Go for a walk. Next, we go for a walk in nature, alone and in silence. The hour or so outside is not a time to think about what we will create or even try to analyze the prompt. It is simply a time to notice. To be present. If a bird sings, I notice. If a boy passes on a bicycle, I notice. If there are interesting seedpods standing tall on thistle stalks, I look at them. Some of the items I see might spur an idea later when I'm working on my collage. Or maybe it's just a nice meditative walk in nature.

Gather collage materials. When we get into the studio, I look through the various containers of images. Maybe I'm drawn to landscapes. I shuffle through them and pull out several that appeal to me. Then I might move on to people or butterflies or artworks or words. I don't try to second-guess how this or that will fit into my collage, or even if it will end up in the collage at all. I just collect images I like, knowing I'm selecting many more than I can possibly use. After I have my images, I wander around the room looking at fabric scraps, ribbons, and trinkets. I may or may not bring some to my work area.

Create a collage. Next comes the arranging of images. Again, I try to do as little analysis as possible. The question at the beginning of the day set the intention. I've written a page or two in response to the question. I've walked in nature and certain things caught my eye. I've selected images that appeal to me. Now it's a matter of allowing my playful child to come forward and make something out of the resources I've selected for her. I need to get out of her way and allow her to play!

While everyone is absorbed in their own creations, there is very little talking. There might be a chuckle or a sigh. Occasionally someone will get up and walk around the room to see what others are doing. But there is little if any distracting chit-chat. The creative energy in the room is focused, sometimes intense, sometimes light, always supportive.

Allow a story to unfold. Visual journaling with collage, in the method I have described, borders on art therapy. Without a doubt it is therapeutic. If I were doing collage as art, I would think carefully about composition, placement, color, texture, and all the other stuff that goes into creating an art piece. Using it as a form of journaling, I want to get out of the thinking mode and just allow things to happen. The end result might look and feel like artwork, might even be quite artistic, but that's not the purpose or the point. It's the story being told that's important. What does my inner self tell me through the pieces I put into my collage? We are not judging our work as capital-*A* Art pieces. We are not judging at all. We are asking our inner self, our five-year-old child, our pain or grief or joy, to speak to us through images.

Sharing our work. We end the day in a circle, following

the guidelines we've agreed on. Each person shares what they have done, what it means to them, and what insights they might have had. Then others in the group respond. Someone might notice something in the collage that resonates with what was said earlier. There are no judgments made or even conclusions drawn. Just a noticing. An echoing back. A mirroring.

No value statements. While it might seem nice to compliment someone on her collage, we have a hard rule against it. This work is not about liking or judging. It makes no difference if you like my finished piece or not. It's what it means to me and what I've learned in the process of making it that matters. We're not writing to please someone else, and we're not collaging for praise. You may mirror or notice something in the collage or make connections to what was said earlier in the morning sharing session, but no judging or drawing conclusions for anyone's work other than your own. And even then, don't judge. Just learn.

Because we're so accustomed to using encouraging language, this can be a hard rule to learn, but very important for insightful work to occur.

Summary

- Meet in circle and agree to guidelines.
- The facilitator presents a question or prompt.
- Write for five to seven minutes in response to the prompt.
- Listen to each other's responses with the understanding that sharing is always optional.
- Allow an hour to walk in nature, alone, in silence. Don't think about the given prompt. Simply notice whatever is present.
- At the given time, meet in the workspace to create a collage.
- With as little analysis as possible, select images that

appeal to you.

- Objects from the natural world might find their way into the collage, becoming symbols with deeper meaning. Don't force it, but allow it to happen.
- Invite your five-year-old self to create, not your analytical, judgmental, perfectionist adult who has specific ideas about what "art" is.
- Meet in circle to share. No judgments allowed, only observations.

NOTE: Individual collages may relate to the prompt or may turn out to be something entirely different that's calling for our attention.

When words become unclear, I shall focus with photographs.
When images become inadequate, I shall be content with silence.
Ansel Adams

CHAPTER 6: VISUAL JOURNALING WITH PHOTOGRAPHY

A ll types of journaling can help us go deeper within our own psyches, help us get clearer on what we believe and who we are. Some journaling techniques have a more outward focus, helping us notice things in the environment, details we might walk by every day without noticing. Photo journaling began like that for me, an outward focus, and then turned inward as well.

The photo-a-day practice is more of an outward approach, while photo journaling is more of a deliberate exploration of thoughts and feelings along with the image taken with the camera. Following are descriptions of how I have used each.

Photo-a-Day

I set an intention to shoot a photo each day for an entire year. It started out pretty easy. I had heard about a woman who limited herself to shooting only in her backyard and house. Now *that* would be hard. After the first dozen shots, you'd run out of the obvious stuff and have to get more and more creative, look at things from different angles and perspectives.

Another photographer, a professional who made his living with his photographs, took the approach of limiting himself to

ONE shot each day for ninety days (Jim Brandenburg, *Chased by the Light*). Think about that! What if you saw something interesting early in the morning, took your shot, and then the most magnificent fox crosses your path that very afternoon. How do you know when you've got the one and only shot you can take that day? (Brandenburg talks about this dilemma in his beautiful book of photographs.)

I didn't put either of those restrictions on myself. While I applaud these two photographers, their ideas were beyond what I was willing to do. I didn't limit my environment nor the number of shots I could take. I could go anywhere and shoot to my heart's content.

When you set a goal of shooting a photo a day, you carry your camera with you always. You are attentive to everything around you. Let me tell you about my incredible experience on Day 2!

I was driving in downtown Dallas and noticed ominous storm clouds in my rearview mirror. I whipped an illegal U-turn into the jail parking lot, parked in a no-parking spot, and grabbed my camera. I left my inner rule-follower speechless and wide-eyed as I jumped over a low fence to get to an open field. There, on a bridge crossing the Trinity river, was a train. With menacing green clouds rushing in, the sky was lit with an iridescent light. I would not miss this perfect shot!

I submitted the photo for judging in the Dallas Camera Club monthly contest. The judge, a photographer on the east coast, marked me down because "there's no such thing as a green sky." He may have been a good photographer, but he didn't know squat about tornadoes. I had a great shot and a good laugh!

Some days were golden with worthy shots everywhere I turned. Other days I struggled. In my enthusiasm, I posted my photo-a-day to Facebook. That kept me accountable, gave me a record of my work, and the feedback was appreciative. Even so, after a few months, I felt like the woman in her backyard, searching for new perspectives, new angles. The challenge became greater with each passing day.

To help with the challenge, I began choosing monthly themes. One month, I chose public art. Like any large city, Dallas has a lot of public art. I had noticed sculptures and admired them, but didn't go out of my way to find them. This is where Facebook came in handy. As I posted pictures of sculptures, friends began telling me of others around town.

Someone told me of a commercial complex north of Dallas that had dozens of sculptures on their grounds, and art pieces in a lobby. Others led me to giant teddy-bear statues in a children's park, leprechauns in another, a tiny oriental-themed park tucked in a busy neighborhood. There were hidden gems all over the area that I never would have found had it not been for this photo-a-day adventure.

For seven weeks, rainbow was my theme. A whole week of shooting nothing but red. The following week, orange. Then yellow, green, blue, indigo, and violet. (You try shooting a whole week of indigo!) I turned it into a guessing game, shooting a whole row of orange wheelbarrow handles lined up at Home Depot, for example. "Who can tell me what this is and where it was shot?"

There were days when I had to grab something before the sun went down or take my chances with a lighted night shot. Not one day, in the entire year, did I go to bed without shooting a photograph. I learned a lot about photography that year, but I also learned to pay more attention to what was going on around me, and to get outdoors and explore my environment.

I also learned some basics about learning:
- Practice something every day and you'll get better. (OR a bad habit is ingrained if you're doing it wrong!)
- Doing the same thing every day gets boring.
- To remain interesting, a challenge needs to get a bit more difficult with each succeeding day.

I also noticed that I miss so much every day. When I shoot red, I see red everywhere! When I shoot public art, I see art everywhere! I see what I pay attention to.

Combining Photography with Writing

In 2008, a friend and I began a photo-journaling adventure where we would shoot a photograph, write a sentence or a paragraph and send them to each other. The result of this adventure was a self-published book we titled *I, Too. Me Neither*.

Following is the introduction to the book. It explains our process and what we learned better than anything I could write today, some dozen years later.

Photo Connecting, Photo Journaling

Way down deep inside, you are a writer. Or at least you'd like to be.

You have thoughts and feelings you'd like to express. You write in spurts. Sometimes the words don't get down on paper. They just stay in paragraphs in your head. Sometimes they gush out and you think you're on the path to a book you might submit to a publisher. Then life gets in the way and you put it away with other "someday, if-only" fantasies. Later, you begin again. A thought here, a line there. You jot down book titles you'd like to write. Sometimes the title is enough.

Some days the words flow freely and time stands still. You enter that zone of creativity where your fingers can't move fast enough to keep up with the river of words. Other times the stream trickles or dries up to nothing. But meanwhile stuff keeps happening and you want a way to process all that stuff. Writing helps. But sometimes writing isn't enough. The words aren't sufficient, or they just don't work. At least, this is the way it is for me.

Parker Palmer talks about "third things." At times we need something outside ourselves to help us talk about the things deepest within ourselves. A poem. A painting. A hike. We need to come at life sideways because it's so slippery and feathery and chaotic that we can't seem to catch it face forward straight on. The feelings are too raw, too elusive, too personal, or too scary. And yet it is those feelings and thoughts that most connect us to each other.

"Oh yeah? I know exactly what you mean. I couldn't quite put my finger on it until you said what you said. I, too! Me, neither."

We—my friend and I—wanted a way to connect. Something fun to do, but "fun with a purpose," we said. We decided to go on a photo excursion. Then we would pick out a couple pictures we liked and write about them. Not write as in "describe," but write as in "journal." What does this photo say to you? What does it make you think about? We had nothing specific in mind. No themes. No agenda.

Our first excursion was a trip to the Arboretum, which offered lots of photo ops. Individually we reviewed our pictures, selected a couple, wrote, and shared. What came out was stuff we were dealing with—chaos, community, friendship, questions, regrets, joy, and grief. Well, all of it didn't come out on that first excursion, but it did come out over time. It was the "third thing" kind of experience: my friend, me, and a third thing that helped the two of us think about, identify, and talk about stuff. It was just for us—a way to explore and connect, to find those I-toos and me-neithers.

We printed a few of our photo-journal pages, and they began to take on a new life. A spouse suggested putting a calendar together. We selected thirteen of our best pages and printed enough calendars for family members and a few friends. The process of putting a calendar together forced us to think deeper, to edit, to be selective. We got such encouraging responses that we wondered if we hadn't stumbled on a way to help people get at those deep soul rumblings.

We kept shooting and writing, and one day decided to print out everything we had done. We had close to 100 photo-journal pages. We cleared off a table and silently walked around it, sorting the pages into clusters. She would put one in one stack, and I would pick it up and put it in another. Some went into the discard pile. Life is like that—all connected and messy and chaotic, and some things we just have to let go.

At some point we had to agree that it would never be perfect, never be finished, always be in process. We settled on six loose clusters. We named them—again trying to understand what it was that we were thinking about, what we were trying to make sense of.

With a dozen or more photos and writings in each cluster, we had a new way of thinking about the topics. We wrote about the topics themselves. That turned the process upside down on its head. We saw things differently out in the visual world. We thought about balance and looked for photos to shoot that spoke about balance. We thought about noticing things and looked for details and light and shadows and joy in children's faces. We thought about tough stuff and looked for ways to express deep grief that we had carried for years.

Originally, we had words with every page, every picture. That's how we figured out what we were trying to say, what we were trying to understand. When we got closer to the center, closer to our own meaning, we found we needed fewer words. We put the project together and gave it to a couple of reviewers. One said she wanted more words with each picture. Another said to use fewer words. A third said to remove the words altogether—let the viewer make up his own interpretation. In the end, we went with our gut: sometimes words, sometimes no words at all.

This is our story. It's not complete. It's not perfect. It is a process. As we share it with you, our hope is that you feel invited into the process.

Here are a few photo- journaling examples from *I, Too. Me Neither.*

Don't mess with me until I've had my mocha latte grande hold-the-whip.

Will my story be so well written?

Jack's body was broken. Dove into a swimming pool and traded his strong, independent body for a wheelchair and mouth-stick. Somehow, he had worked through his losses by the time I met him. He nourished and changed my life as he did for so many others. I loved his smile. I loved his spirit. He was one of the most able people I've ever known.

Summary: Photo-a-Day

- Shoot a photo each day for a whole year.
- Post to social media as a form of accountability and a means of interacting with others.
- Experiment with shooting themes.

Summary: Photo Journaling

- Let the picture tell the story as much as possible.
- Write only short paragraphs or single sentences.
- Write first and then shoot.
- Shoot first and then write.

AFTERWORD

Living a less purposeful life. That's what my friend told me she was going to do: live her life based on what was satisfying and quit trying to make everything meaningful. Something moved in me. The light shifted. I had struggled all my life with *meaningful* and *purposeful*. Instead of doing something just for the sheer enjoyment of it, there always had to be a purpose, a meaning. And *meaning* was so heavy and serious and unfulfilling because it was never meaningful *enough*. It never solved some big world problem. Never even came close. Anything I did achieve only showed me how much more there was to do. I was on an unending challenge course being mocked by my internal judge saying, "Not enough, not enough, never enough." Meaning/purpose was my task-master.

Wasn't it time to let go of having to have anything and everything be *meaningful*, and to be content with what was simply *satisfying*?

Satisfying: fulfilling, delightful, enjoyable, favorable, gratifying, hitting the spot, pleasant, pleasing, refreshing, rewarding, satiating, satisfactory, savory, sweet.

Meaningful: significant, consequential, eloquent, essential, important, momentous, purposeful, relevant, serious, substantial, useful, valid, weighty, worthwhile.

Meaningful revolves around achievement. *Satisfying* revolves around joy—quiet or exuberant or anywhere in between. And what is *joy*?

Joy: great happiness, pleasure, comfort, delight, gladness, good humor, gratification, jubilance, refreshment, satisfaction, solace, treat, treasure, wonder. Joy has a wide range of expression from jubilant to quiet. When I think of the jubilant end of the spectrum, I think of children. In fact, though, children express both ends from jubilant to quiet wonder. How do we lose that childlike joy?

For me, I think it was because I had absorbed the message so thoroughly that everything had to have meaning.

"That's enough foolishness. Time to get to work."

"But what's it good for?"

"Don't waste precious time."

Even an outdoor excursion had to have a purpose: to find certain geological specimens. Not just any rock would do. Consider the smooth, yellowish-brown stone my six-year-old sister found one time. Proud of her treasure, she showed it off, only to be told it was nothing. *Nothing.* It was nothing since it didn't fit the declared purpose of the excursion.

My heart hurt as I thought of *meaning* and how a child's spirit could be bruised and scarred by its heaviness. If it doesn't have a purpose, is it not worth doing? (Maybe as a thumbing-my-nose at that serious rock-collecting excursion, today I collect "nothing rocks." Many are shaped like hearts and they bring me joy!)

Today I look at my list of satisfying things and realize how it's so different from the one I used to keep, the one where each item had to have achievement attached to it in order to justify the time spent on it. Even a hobby had to have a purpose, and it had to be a grander purpose than merely enjoyment or relaxation. Do you begin to see how difficult it was for me to embrace my artist? With so many problems in the world and so much *IMPORTANT* stuff to do, how dare I waste time on stringing beads, shaping a pot, taking a photograph, or watercoloring?

Through lots and lots of journaling, and searching, and seeking help from wise people along the way, I finally came to the realization that I was never going to solve some major world problem, and furthermore, that was okay. It was a weight off my shoulders the day I took off my heavy armor and mask, and embraced the child, the artist, the seeker, the wanderer, the mentor, the writer; and reined in the judge, the addict of busyness, the victim, and even the good girl times ten.

In the end, I had to redefine *meaning*. Not as the stuffy, serious, self-important one dressed in a black suit with proper shoes feeling responsible for solving every problem that came along. *Meaning* could be spreading *joy* and *beauty* and *gratitude*, intangibles that could ripple out and touch someone who touched someone who perhaps solved some important problem. Or made the world a little more loving.

It hasn't been easy. When certain beliefs and rules are so deeply ingrained, they cut a deep rut in the brain. Transformation is not an overnight thing. It's a process, a spiral, a journey. Certainly, some people have instant transformations. It wasn't that way for me. It was, and sometimes continues to be, a day-by-day struggle. If I wasted a whole day, I turned inward, became depressed. I felt like I let someone down. Sometimes I became panicky because time was slipping away. What had I done? What had I accomplished? What difference had I made?

It was journaling that helped more than anything else to get me out of the *achievement/purpose* rut of living my life and see other ways of being in the world. Other ways that fit so much better with who I was at the deepest level, who I was at the soul level. It took spiraling around topics and beliefs using journaling of so many different types.

We've scratched the surface here as I've introduced you to the various techniques that helped me so much. For any technique you are drawn to, there are many more mentors and teachers who can take you further. I've included some in *References and Resources*. There are dozens of others, as well as many other ways to journal. (We didn't even touch on poetry, for example. John Fox, *Finding What You Didn't Lose*, is an excellent resource for that. And did I mention that Naomi Shihab Nye is one of my favorite poets?)

My hope is that sharing the work I've done provides an overview of several possibilities to help you dig deeper into your own hidden parts, challenge your unchallenged assumptions, and discover things you never suspected about yourself. There's a beautiful soul inside each of us waiting to be discovered.

Part 3:
Good to Know

ADDITIONAL JOURNALING TECHNIQUES

Ask a Question

Ask a question and wait. Don't just automatically begin writing. Let the question sit lonely at the top of the page. Breathe. Count to twenty. Good questions deserve a little solo time on stage. Admire the question and your courage to ask it. Now write. Do not judge, evaluate, or analyze. Just write what comes in response to the question.

Ask "Why?" Five Times

- Start with a question. Then write no more than a two-sentence answer.
- Next write *Why did I say that?* Answer in one sentence.
- Next write *Why did I say that?* Again, answer in one sentence.
- Repeat *Why did I say that?* five times. You might be surprised at your final answer. Often it leads to the motivation underneath the initial question and answer.

Please note: At no time can you answer with *Because I said so.*

Use Prompts

Almost every article on journaling or self-help book has prompts for you to answer. Pick and choose the ones that appeal to you and write for your eyes only. If your intention is to find the person under the layers of masks and costumes, keep your writing private. Even well-meaning friends might want to fix you, assure you, help you, answer your questions for you, or explain the way it really is. This is you exploring you, not you seeking approval or acceptance.

Interview Someone, Living or Dead

Sit down in a comfortable chair with another chair facing you. Invite the person of interest to join you. This can be anyone: a famous person you've always wanted to meet, an historical person long gone but living on in your imagination, even a character from literature. The point is to imagine that person in the chair facing you. Imagine as clearly as possible using everything you know about him or her. Put yourself in their shoes, their clothing, their time, their circumstances.

Now start a dialog. You are both the interviewer and the interviewee. Ask a question you've always wanted to ask. Then pause long enough to become that person of interest. Change chairs if it helps. Answer the question as if the other person is speaking. You many be surprised by what flows from your pen.

- Who would you like to talk to?
- What would you ask?
- How would he or she answer?

This is a journaling technique that becomes easier and more meaningful with practice. Don't forget that interviews can also be conducted with your archetypes and shadows.

Use Your Nondominant Hand

This is hard and takes practice and patience. It's well worth the effort. Often your nondominant hand presents an entirely different perspective. My left hand puts words and concepts together that are surprising and fun, quite different from my more analytical right hand.

If you're intrigued by this idea, check out *The Power of Your Other Hand* by Lucia Capacchione.

MANDALAS ALL AROUND US

Once you become aware of mandalas, you'll see them everywhere. In my childhood, I was drawn to kaleidoscopes and spirographs. In high school, I loved the patterns and symmetry of geometry. When I found mandalas, I stumbled onto an artform that became both a meditative and a journaling practice. I had discovered, like many before me, a spiritual practice that crosses cultural lines. From the Buddhist sand mandalas to the Rose Windows of the cathedrals, to the Navajo healing mandalas, to the ancient labyrinths, people have been drawn to mandalas across the ages in deep, meaningful ways. Mother Nature was the first artist, creating with geometric repetitive patterns that often result in mandalas.

Creating Photo Mandalas in Photoshop

There are many computer programs that will create photo mandalas from your photos. I like the slower method of creating them step by step in Photoshop and watching them evolve. The basic procedures (requiring a working knowledge of using layers in Photoshop) are as follows:

Using a self-created template with the appropriate number of degrees in the triangle (must divide equally into 360), I "cut" a triangle from the original photograph and put it into a new file. Then I duplicate the triangle and flip the copy so it is a mirror image of the first one. I line them up carefully and join them, making them one image. Then I duplicate this image and follow the same procedure of flipping and joining until I have a complete circle. See following page for visual directions.

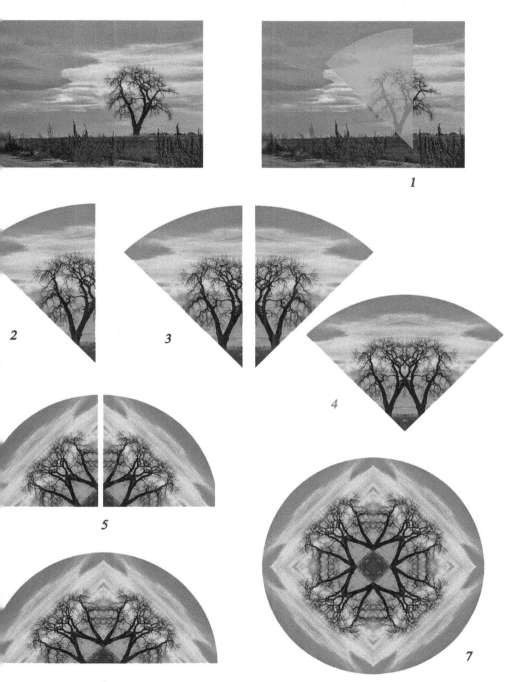

1

2

3

4

5

6

7

Drawing Mandalas

Mandalas can be drawn free form by drawing a circle, dividing it into equal sections and adding designs within the sections. Or you might want to use a compass and experiment with designing them very symmetrically. A protractor and a straight edge are also handy for dividing a circle into equal parts.

There are many different basic mandalas that can be drawn with a compass. A good one to start with is the six-petal mandala as shown here:

1. Using a compass, draw a circle.
2. Without changing the radius of the compass, put the metal tip of the compass on the circle (point 1) and draw an arc.
3. The arc will touch the circle at two points. Put the metal tip on one of the points (point 2) and draw the next arc. This arc will touch the circle at points 1 and 3.
4. Put the metal tip at point 3 and draw the next arc. Continue around the circle until you have six petals.
5. Embellish the petals.

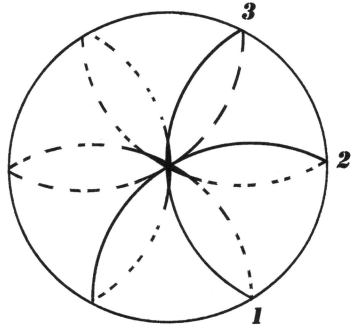

SUGGESTED CIRCLE GUIDELINES

A circle is not a discussion group. It's a structure and a process to encourage people to get in touch with their deepest selves. Participants should never feel like they have to defend themselves but rather should feel free to speak their truth as they know it without fear of judgment. A circle is a place to speak our questions out loud—not to seek answers from anyone else, but so we can hear them, own them, and wonder about them. There is no fixing or setting anyone straight. Just listening with open hands and open hearts. A circle is based on the premise that, deep inside, we have our own answers. We just need safe ways and places to explore them. I have learned about circles from various authors and mentors (Deming's Quality Circles; David Langford's work based on Deming; Parker Palmer's Circles of Trust; Courage and Renewal retreats, retreats led by facilitators trained by Christina Baldwin.)

The following are not original but have been modified to express my understanding of the most helpful guidelines.

1. Be fully present to the people in the circle and be fully present yourself.
2. Leave the outside world outside. No cell phones, no to-do lists, no schedules. This is a set-aside time to *Be fully present*.
3. Listen without judgment. This is not a place for arguing a point or even disagreeing. It's a place where people should feel comfortable to speak from their deepest self without fear.
4. Speak only for yourself. No "we-ing."
5. Speak to the center of the circle with no crosstalk. Don't respond to what someone else has said; just listen respectfully.

6. Using a "talking piece" can be helpful. Only the person holding the piece may speak.

7. Silence is okay. In fact, silence is welcomed as a member of the circle. This can be uncomfortable at first since we are so used to filling silence. It gets easier with practice.

8. Participation is by invitation only. No one should feel pressured to share. "Pass" is always an option.

9. Share in ways that respect others' truths.

10. Honor confidentiality at all times.

11. Open and close the circle with a simple ritual that marks the time as dedicated to the purpose. For example, light and extinguish a candle, or ring a chime.

REFERENCES AND RESOURCES

Bearden, Donna and Kathleen Martin. *I, Too. Me Neither: A photo-journaling experience with my friend*. Dallas: self-published, 2008.

Bradbury, Ray. *Zen in the Art of Writing: Essays on Creativity*. Santa Barbara, CA: Capra Press, 1990.

Brandenburg, Jim. *Chased by the Light*. Minnetonka, Minnesota: NorthWord Press, 1998.

Brown, Brené. *The Gifts of Imperfection: Let go of who you think you're supposed to be and embrace who you are*. Center City, Minnesota: Hazelden, 2010.

Cameron, Julia. *The Artist's Way: A spiritual path to higher creativity*. New York: Jeremy P. Tarcher/Putnam, Inc., 1992.

Cameron, Julia. *The Right to Write: An invitation and initiation into the writing life*. New York: Jeremy P. Tarcher/Putnam, Inc., 1998.

Capacchione, Lucia. *The Power of Your Other Hand*. Franklin Lakes, NJ: The Career Press, Inc., 2001.

Chödrön, Pema. *Compassion Cards: teachings for awakening the heart in everyday life*. Boulder, CO: Shambala Publications, Inc., 2016.

Ford, Debbie. *The Dark Side of the Light Chasers: Reclaiming your power, creativity, brilliance, and dreams*. New York: Riverhead Books, 1998.

Fox, Matthew. *One River, Many Wells: Wisdom springing from global faiths*. New York: Jeremy P. Tarcher/Putnam, Inc., 2000.

Fox, John. *Finding What You Didn't Lose: Expressing your truth and creativity through poem making*. New York: G.P. Putnam's Sons, 1995.

Gelb, Michael J. *How to Think Like Leonardo da Vinci: Seven steps to genius every day.* New York: Delacorte Press, 1998.

Gilbert, Elizabeth. *Big Magic: Creative living beyond fear.* New York: Riverhead, 2015.

Lamott, Anne. *Bird by Bird: Some instructions on writing and life.* New York: Doubleday, 1994.

Jones, Laurie Beth. *The Path: Creating your mission statement for work and for life.* New York: Hyperion, 1996.

Maslow, Abraham H. *Toward a Psychology of Being,* second edition. Princeton, New Jersey: D. Van Nostrand Company, Inc., 1962.

Myss, Carolyn. *Sacred Contracts.* New York: Harmony Books, 2001.

Palmer, Parker. *A Hidden Wholeness: The journey toward an undivided life.* San Francisco: Jossey-Bass, 2004.

Palmer, Parker. *Let Your Life Speak: Listening for the voice of vocation.* San Francisco: Jossey-Bass, 2000.

Pearson, Carol S. *Awakening the Heroes Within: Twelve archetypes to help us find ourselves and transform the world.* San Francisco: HarperSanFrancisco, 1991.

Pennebaker, James W. *Opening Up: The healing power of expressing emotions.* New York, London: The Guilford Press, 1990.

Progoff, Ira. *At a Journal Workshop: Writing to access the power of the unconscious and evoke creative ability (Revised).* New York: Jeremy P. Tarcher/Putnam, Inc., 1975, 1992.

Stone, Sidra. *The Shadow King: The invisible force that holds women back.* Lincoln, NE: iUniverse.com, Inc., 1997.

Tyler, Kathy and Joy Drake. *The Original Angel Cards: Inspirational Messages and Meditations.* InnerLinks Associates, 2006.

ACKNOWLEDGEMENTS

I did not know how difficult writing acknowledgements could be. Where in a lifetime do you start? Where does a story begin? When does learning start? Everything I've done, experienced, or written has been influenced and helped by more people than I could name. Everyone who has ever touched my life, whether in positive or challenging ways, I learned from you and am grateful.

To my life-long partner who has loved, supported and believed in me, thanks to Leighton Bearden. I could grow because you were and continue to be my safe place and so much more.

To my long-time friend, adventurer, encouraging supporter, and fellow writer, Rebecca Bruff, many thanks.

To my fine-tooth comb manuscript readers, Sally Hare and Elsie Wood, who offered suggestions and edits, I owe you a huge debt of gratitude.

To Jim Rogers who read the manuscript and suggested the title, thank you.

To Elaine Sullivan, an incredible counselor and human being, who unblocked my energy, unstuck my stuckness, held me accountable, challenged me to grow, I cannot say thank you enough.

Thank you to Parker Palmer, Cindy Johnson, and all the Courage and Renewal facilitators who are living examples of what they teach: how to live an undivided life, the same on the outside as on the inside. From them I learned to listen deeper, ask better questions, and trust that each person has an internal teacher. This, more than anything, is what journaling is to me. Communicating with my own internal teacher. Getting quiet enough to listen to the deepest part of me.

And thank you to all the creatives at Koehler Books. Encouraging, thoughtful, inspiring. You are a gift to writers.

CPSIA information can be obtained
at www.ICGtesting.com
Printed in the USA
LVHW052343100720
660319LV00007B/150